Raising Intentional Parents

Jennifer Jensen
with contributions from
GatheringFamilies.com

ISBN-10: 1542966213
ISBN-13: 978-1542966214

Table of Contents

Forward

My journey to find and emulate great parents began before I had any children of my own. My family did not provide the ideal setting and this left me with the desire to look for better examples to emulate. I'm sure my parents had great hopes for our family and even greater dreams. But when reality hit with children, bills, and all that happens in a family, those dreams didn't survive for long. With a family history of mental illnesses, different forms of abuse, and a lack of good role models, they just didn't have the recipe for parenting success. I was left with a sense of desperation to find role models whose ideas I could follow and incorporate into my future family. Consequently, I was drawn to parents and families I could see were different.

When I found a family with great kids and that special spirit about them, I tried to watch and learn while paying close attention to their parenting style. Some of the things I was curious about were: how they taught their children, what they taught, how they disciplined, what family activities they shared, and how they interacted as a couple. These families gladly shared their experiences with me and I will always be grateful for their help. When my husband and I began our own family later on, all the ideas I gathered from these wonderful families helped me choose a better path to follow.

A few years ago, a friend introduced me to the amazing ideas behind GatheringFamilies.com. This group was founded by some amazing moms who wanted to be Intentional Parents and it has grown into a large support group for moms and even some dads. Their mission statement is full of important truths. One example is:

> Gathering Families seeks to foster relationships among families who are striving to impart a Biblical worldview to their children in order to help them fully *"learn and live the gospel."* These children will be the next generation of defenders of the natural family and must be able to articulate and defend the truths espoused in *The Family: A Proclamation to the World* in their families and in the public square with conviction and compassion.

I met many moms who are part of Gathering Families at the World Congress of Families held in Salt Lake City, Utah in 2015. Between meetings, we brainstormed about how we could best help families around the world catch a glimpse of their amazing potential. Our discussions centered around such topics as: how to help the next generation prepare to take their roles as parents seriously, how to strengthen our youth to help them stay strong and faithful in an ever-worsening world, how to inspire others to join us in this effort, and how to bring the focus back to the family as the fundamental unit of society. We all recognized that nothing can replace the family, and yet many powerful groups are trying.

As we discussed the idea of parenting with purpose and thought for the future—even intentionally—we realized that this really isn't a common practice anymore. People's lives are so busy; we are pulled in many directions every day and parenting often gets pushed to the side as, seemingly, more urgent matters turn our attention elsewhere. For more than a generation now, parents have focused less and less on their children which means rising generations are not being taught what it means to "parent." Today, parenting has evolved into something that looks more like providing for material wants and scheduling activities instead of teaching good morals and principles. While parents are focusing on providing for their children's physical needs, organizations are stepping in to take over the role of teaching principles and values to their children. But are the principles these organizations teach the same ones parents believe in?

These discussions were the spark that led me to compile this book, *Raising Intentional Parents*. It was written to cover two important topics:

- Choosing to parent with intent and making it the priority God intended it to be, and
- Recognizing that we can prepare our children to be faithful, committed parents when they have families of their own.

My goal was to bring good parenting ideas together with personal experiences shared from parents in Gathering Families. I would like to thank each of them who shared their personal experiences. I believe these stories will help many moms and dads focus on parenting by principle and on centering their homes on what matters most—the truths of eternity.

Now, as my children are almost grown and I have entered that idyllic realm of being a grandma, I realize just how much I would have benefited from a book like this when I was a new parent. I hope the stories that are shared here will help you along your own journey to becoming an Intentional Parent and raising future Intentional Parents from generation to generation.

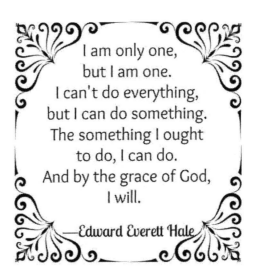

I am only one,
but I am one.
I can't do everything,
but I can do something.
The something I ought
to do, I can do.
And by the grace of God,
I will.

—Edward Everett Hale

The Idea of Intentional Parenting

For behold, this is my work and my glory —
to bring to pass the immortality and eternal life of man.

— Moses 1:39

Our Heavenly Father intentionally placed us in this mortal experience to give us the opportunities we need to return to Him. According to this scripture, we are not merely a side job but *the* job, His only work. What an amazing idea he had for us to learn and grow! This life is full of hands-on experiences, consequences, and learning moments. On top of it all, we get to help some of God's other children learn and grow as well: we get to be parents.* We shouldn't look at our role of helping with His work as any less important than He sees His own work. We are helping "to bring to pass the immortality and eternal life"

---

* We will always discuss the God-ordained traditional nuclear family with His ideas of their various responsibilities. We might not all have this family form but we can work towards it and we can teach our children to aim for this as well.

of ourselves, our children, and any other lives we may touch.

If this is true, the most important work of mothers and fathers is to bring our children to a knowledge of God and His Plan of Salvation, enabling them to return to their Heavenly Parents. As I think about this responsibility, several thoughts come to mind: if God is deliberate and intentional as he accomplishes His work, shouldn't I be intentional in my own parenting work as well? And if my husband and I are to be successful in our parenting endeavors, shouldn't our goals match His goals?

But there's another side to our responsibility of raising good children: we as parents need to return to Him as well. Again, our Heavenly Father thought of everything. In all His wisdom, God made the benefits of parenting help both children and parents, allowing all of us to learn the most from our individual experiences. Helping God accomplish His goals for our children accomplishes His goals for us at the same time. No one learns better than when they are teaching it themselves. This means we, as parents, are enrolled in a sort of Parenting 101 class. We get our first taste or experience in parenting here which can continue into the next life if we are worthy.

This means we must have a goal or a plan in which we can see all the desired outcomes. It must be a stronger motivation than the desire to give up on bad days or coast on good days. It has to be right out in front always leading us on if we are to reach those amazing heights. With a vision of our goals in mind, we have direction, incentive to work hard, and a way to make it through tough times. Without that, there is no way we can keep going in the face of the opposition we experience in this journey. This is what intentional means—intent on reaching the goal of raising righteous children who are prepared to do the same.

The young men who were part of the Army of Helaman did not have the amazing spiritual experiences their parents had of being taught by Ammon, burying their weapons, and choosing to die rather than sin again. But somehow their parents were still able to pass on that knowledge to them.[1] In other scripture stories this didn't always happen. What a difference between these young men and the ones who lived during the reign of King Benjamin who were too young to understand his great speech: many of that rising generation rejected his words.[2]

Of course there is no way to guarantee children's testimonies will always grow the way we would like, but if parents couldn't make a difference, then God wouldn't bother designing parents and families into His plan. However, He did design it that way because parenting *does* make a difference and Intentional Parenting can make an even bigger difference.

> No other work transcends that of righteous, intentional parenting!
> — Russell M. Nelson

Intentional Parenting can be defined as:

> Deliberately choosing to raise children in an environment created to instill a desire for truth, a strong faith in Christ, and a determination to follow Him.

Intentional Parenting means children are the priority. Too often in today's society, they are a side note to adult activities. Our children need to be the main reason we do everything. Raising good children while learning to be good parents is the biggest part we play in Heavenly Father's plan.

I once heard a popular conservative radio host ask parents to find out what their children have learned from

3

them by asking one simple question, "What do we, your parents, most want you to be: successful, smart, good, or happy?"[3] How many children would answer "good"? As it turns out not very many. In fact, most children choose all the other answers before selecting good. This is an interesting impression of parenting today.

Good parenting means making goals and, typically, goals we make are measured in the length of time it takes before they can be achieved. This goal of raising children to successfully return to our Heavenly Father is just about the longest goal imaginable. Often long-range goals can fall through the cracks when there are pressing short-term goals that need addressing. But when it comes to parenting, sometimes those short-term goals can actually get in the way or even hurt the prospects of achieving the long-term goals.

When my children reached an age to begin helping with jobs around our home, many times I told myself it would be a lot easier to just do it myself. My three-year-old helping empty the garbage often meant I was picking up dropped pieces of trash; my six- or seven-year-old helping me clean the bathtub or vacuum the family room meant spending time with touch-ups, pulling toys and stray socks out of the vacuum, or even vacuuming again which felt very much like wasting valuable time already in such short supply.

Two of my short-term goals, accomplishing these tasks quickly and efficiently and having a clean house, were being undermined by little helping hands. But while I was despairing of ever reaching these goals, my big picture, long-term goal of helping my children return to God was working great! My children were learning the valuable skill of hard work and the satisfaction that comes from it. Depending on which goal I focused on, I could either feel very successful or an abject failure. As I tried patiently and lovingly to teach my children these various tasks, I could just imagine the patience and self-control it takes for our Heavenly Father to watch and wait for His work to be accomplished.*

Today, society cares only about short-term goals. For at least a generation, adults have placed parenting on the back burner while they focus on jobs, recreation, and self-fulfillment—all short-term goals. No longer seeing marriage and family as practically synonymous, couples are choosing to have children only after they experience successful careers and years of fun. Goals and dreams have increasingly become about the individual adults rather than the family. And often when couples do decide to have children, day care and latch-keys are the norm.

It is very easy to allow society to distract parents from their parental responsibilities. We are told adults have their "own lives" and parenting is only one aspect. Since it brings no recognition, parenting ends up low on the list of priorities. Working extra hours to secure a raise or promotion brings much more acknowledgement than staying home and raising children. Both parents working so they can afford boats, vacations, or big houses, brings approval from the world. Raising a child doesn't.

President Spencer W. Kimball warned of allowing other interests to replace parenting:

Do not, however, make the mistake of being drawn off into secondary tasks which will cause the

---

neglect of your eternal assignments such as giving birth to and rearing the spirit children of our Father in Heaven. Pray carefully over all your decisions.[4]

A friend of mine began home schooling a couple years ago. She commented to me on how her attitude about mothering has changed considerably since then. She now feels much more responsibility for her children. Mothering is more than just feeding, clothing, and giving them a home. She feels responsible for everything now—education, training, socializing, love, and faith; really everything. But did she ever not have that responsibility or did she just not realize it?

Today many adults, raised without a solid foundation themselves, are perpetuating the same sort of parenting style in which they were raised. This is leading to an increasing number of children alienated from faith-based moral teachings. The proof is in the statistics: just search online for data on single parent households, teen pregnancies, crime rates, school drop-out rates, test scores, abortion rates, gangs, drug abuse, and so on. These examples show how rapidly Intentional Parenting skills are disappearing.

I come from a fairly dysfunctional family. Both my parents did too. I'm guessing this has perpetuated itself for a few generations. The dysfunction in my generation has appeared in a sister who has not spoken with any of the rest of us for over 16 years . . . yes, 16 years! My husband also comes from a dysfunctional family. His father was an alcoholic and his grandfather was an alcoholic and his great grandfather and so on as far back as we know. We got married before really comparing notes, but when we did it was an eye opener for both of us. The really big questions would come a couple years later when I found out I was expecting our first child. How could we break this cycle and raise a generation completely different from any before including our own? Was it possible to raise our children without all that dysfunction? Where could we turn for guidance and good role models?

There are still many good parenting role models out there though they are not always nearby. If we want to be successful and break bad cycles, we need to find those role models and return to parenting as our first priority, to give children the attention, love, and guidance they need. Bad generational cycles can be broken if one generation becomes Intentional Parents.

Parents who understand the importance of placing their children first, instilling morals, and teaching faith can stop generational dysfunction.

> And all thy children shall be taught of the Lord; and great shall be the peace of thy children.
> — Isaiah 54:13

Sometimes it's easy to believe raising great kids happens automatically or without much effort. Our society acts as though somehow it is fate or destiny guiding our children and not parenting. Some of that might be true since agency definitely plays a role, but parents have much more impact than most of us ever realize.

Today governments are trying to adopt an ever greater proportion of the responsibilities previously left to parents. It is increasingly more common to hear things such as, "children belong to the community,"[5] government has a stake in parenting, or *It Takes a Village* to raise a child.[6] Even local governments are getting in on the act. I can't help but believe this is dysfunction breeding more dysfunction. Governments cannot take the place of good parents. No sitter, no teacher, no government worker, and no daycare worker love our children as much as we do and won't have God's help like we can.

Over the years, many people have been happy to let governments ease their parental burdens. Parenting is hard and allowing governments to assist can be a relief. But "assisting" has more and more become "taking over" as parents allow the encroachment to continue. Providing, protecting, educating, training, feeding, and housing are some ways governments are getting involved. But does it fit in with God's plan for us when we continually turn more and more of our parental responsibilities over to governments?

The *Family Proclamation* teaches of the importance a father has to preside, provide, and protect.[7] These are things many governments already do. A mother has the primary responsibility of nurturing her children.[8] Many governments would like to take care of that too. But a large part of nurturing and caring for children is teaching them good principles and truths as well as morals and values to use as guidelines for future actions. Even a cursory knowledge of current events, or a look at the current education standards, will show governments are not teaching the same principles and morals which good parents teach.

Even if parents could believe government programs are doing a fine job raising their children, the other half of the equation isn't getting done. Those parents are not learning the parenting traits they need; remember the Parenting 101 class? This training, learning to be parents like our Father in Heaven, is being neglected. Parents cannot expect to automatically know good parenting skills anymore than they can automatically understand Einstein's Theory of Relativity or how to pilot a plane. Learning,

8

practicing, making mistakes, and trying again are all part of His plan for our improvement.

Too often we don't want to be different or stand out. We end up waiting for others to lead the way in order to not feel alone. In today's world that isn't going to happen. We must have the vision and desire to begin Intentional Parenting even when no one else is doing it. And chances are, once others see us dare to follow our principles, they may dare to as well. President Kimball taught:

> Much of the major growth that is coming to the Church in the last days will come because many of the good women of the world . . . will be drawn to the Church in large numbers. This will happen to the degree that the women of the Church reflect righteousness and articulateness in their lives and to the degree that the women of the Church are seen as distinct and different—in happy ways—from the women of the world.[9]

Our children need us to stand up and take our places as Intentional Parents. We can be that righteous example President Kimball mentioned.

Ronald Reagan made this statement about freedom but it is applicable to virtually every true principle and moral teaching:

> Freedom is never more than one generation away from extinction. We didn't pass it to our children in the bloodstream. It must be fought for, protected, and handed on for them to do the same, or one day we will spend our sunset years telling our children and our children's children what it was once like in the United States where men were free.[10]

This is prophetic and speaks to much more than just freedom; it is true of all principles including those of Intentional Parenting. Because parents understand and live concepts such as faith, sacrifice, discipline, hard work, and diligence does not mean their children will automatically learn them. These attributes are always "one generation away from extinction" and must be intentionally protected, preserved, and passed on. Anything less means our children or our grandchildren might one day be without them. In an age where all good principles, morals, and values have been expunged from society, the only ones capable of teaching these principles are parents who intentionally choose to do so.

Nephi and Jacob understood this:

> And we did magnify our office unto the Lord, taking upon us the responsibility, answering the sins of the people upon our own heads if we did not teach them the work of God with all diligence; wherefore, by laboring with our might their blood might not come upon our garments . . . and we would not be found spotless at the last day.[11]

I have often thought of this scripture and how much these men did for their families and their people. Am I trying that hard with my children so their blood won't be on my hands?

We're going against the world here. But isn't this what Christ said would happen if we followed Him? Really, that's what this is, and more. We're not only following Him; we're also trying to make sure, as much as we can, that our children will also follow Him and our grandchildren as well. It is a multi-generational goal which only God can ensure. I can do my part but then my children have to do theirs—which means they have to understand

10

the multi-generational aspect as well—and their children and so on. This means not only are parents teaching their children to be righteous people, they are also emphasizing how important it is for them to teach their children to be great people too.

We can't fix the world or even our own communities, but we can choose to be Intentional Parents and raise our children with the long range goal of their becoming Intentional Parents themselves to continue the cycle another generation. Nothing else should matter as much. Then when my children (and their children) are asked if their parents want them to be successful, smart, good, or happy, their answer will be, "To be good; to gain eternal life and to pass this knowledge on to my children through my own Intentional Parenting."

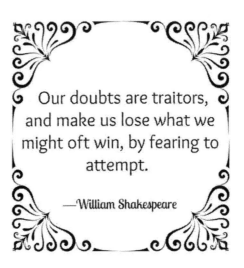

Our doubts are traitors, and make us lose what we might oft win, by fearing to attempt.

—William Shakespeare

Preparation
for the Unknown

When people hear the word preparation, they think "to do" lists, college degrees, or perhaps "Preppers" who store supplies for disasters. None of these are inherently bad or foolish at all, but preparation for being an Intentional Parent and raising another generation of Intentional Parents is a bit less straightforward than writing a grocery list or taking a class.

A couple preparing for the birth of their first child can arrange the nursery and stock up on diapers, blankets, and even some toys, but how would they prepare for a personality they don't know yet or future talents they can only dream about? This excited couple has no way of knowing if their baby will be high maintenance, easy going, or any of a huge number of other personality traits. How do any of us really prepare for such a vast unknown?

Nephi is the quintessential example of being prepared for anything and everything:

> And it came to pass that I, Nephi, said unto my
> father: I will go and do the things which the Lord
> hath commanded, for I know that the Lord giveth no
> commandments unto the children of men, save he

shall prepare a way for them that they may accomplish the thing which he commandeth them.[12]

Nephi knew the Lord would help him do anything He required. He didn't know what all those requirements would be, but Nephi was prepared to follow Christ in whatever He asked. We see great examples of this in the opening pages of the *Book of Mormon*. The story of Nephi trying to get the Brass Plates from Laban is one example of being prepared to follow the Lord no matter what: "And I was led by the Spirit, not knowing beforehand the things which I should do. Nevertheless I went forth. . . ."[13] Nephi had no idea what he was getting into but went willingly anyway. Sometimes parenting is a lot like that. Parents plan and prepare and try to do everything they can but then something completely unexpected can occur.

> We should remember that good fortune often happens when opportunity meets with preparation.
> — Thomas A. Edison

I'm sure Nephi never thought when he was young, "I might have to build a ship all by myself someday; I better learn how." Nothing he personally could have done would have helped with the challenges he faced later on such as getting the Brass Plates, killing Laban, building a ship, leading the righteous in his family, or building a new community from scratch, just to name a few. It doesn't look like he got specific preparation or training in any of these areas as a child. But the preparation he did get was much better. His preparation taught him to follow every spiritual inspiration he received even when he didn't know what might happen.

When the Lord asked Nephi to build a ship, Nephi didn't ask how or get upset God wanted him to do something hard. He didn't even ask where the nearest home

14

improvement center was, thinking he could easily purchase the needed supplies. (Definitely something I would think of.) Nephi trusted God to show him how and immediately acted on that, not expecting it to be quick or painless, but with the faith to know God believed in him and he could believe in God:

> And it came to pass that after I, Nephi, had been in the land of Bountiful for the space of many days, the voice of the Lord came unto me, saying: Arise, and get thee into the mountain. And it came to pass that I arose and went up into the mountain, and cried unto the Lord.
>
> And it came to pass that the Lord spake unto me, saying: Thou shalt construct a ship, after the manner which I shall show thee, that I may carry thy people across these waters.
>
> And I said: Lord, whither shall I go that I may find ore to molten, that I may make tools to construct the ship after the manner which thou hast shown unto me?
>
> And it came to pass that the Lord told me whither I should go to find ore, that I might make tools.[14]

Nephi recognized some of the steps necessary for building a ship but the Lord showed him how to do it. He knew the Lord would help him but he didn't expect it to be easy. I don't know about you but I wouldn't be asking about ore or tools, I would be offering my idea of an already finished ship just appearing one morning like the Liahona. Nephi had a completely different mindset; he was ready to work hard. Parenting can be like that: we would love it if our children were amazing without a lot of hard work on our part, but Intentional Parents understand all that hard work is completely worth it in the end.

> *A scripture I always return to when I think of preparing to be a parent is D&C 88:118-119:*
> *"And as all have not faith, seek ye diligently and teach one another words of wisdom; yea, seek ye out of the best books words of wisdom; seek learning, even by study and also by faith.*
> *"Organize yourselves; prepare every needful thing; and establish a house, even a house of prayer, a house of fasting, a house of faith, a house of learning, a house of glory, a house of order, a house of God. . . ."[15]*
> *This is the goal for my home. I might not ever actually make it but it's still my goal. Preparing for something unknown is hard. This scripture gave me a goal I can understand, picture in my mind, and work towards.*

One of the best ways to prepare for Intentional Parenting actually begins with strengthening marriage first. We are told many times in the scriptures: "Therefore shall a man leave his father and his mother, and shall cleave unto his wife: and they shall be one flesh."[16] It is necessary for a husband and wife to learn to work together as a team. This is a much better option than each doing their own thing, opposing each other, or competing with each other. Couples won't always see eye to eye or completely agree on many issues, but trying to work together and appearing in agreement in front of their children is the important part. Kids need to see mom and dad as a united front.

As a couple decides to start a family, they should discuss parenting, rules, discipline, holiday traditions, etc. If these things are decided ahead of time, the actual transition into parenting can be much easier. As the children grow, parents need to keep communicating and working together. Those who don't will be pitted against each other. As children get older, they quickly figure out which parent is more lenient or easier to manipulate and exactly how to get away with it. Working together, parents can strengthen each other as they stay united. If children know that rules and discipline are consistent with both mom and dad, the challenges of parenting will decrease dramatically.

When parents keep close to the Spirit and each other, the answers will come when they are needed most. Taking a leap of faith will sometimes be a necessary part of Intentional Parenting. Sometimes preparation means preparing for those times when we don't know what to do, but that's how parenting works.

There are examples of excellent family relationships in good books and in the scriptures as well as in society. The last chapter contains a list of books with good marriage and family examples. This would be a good place to start. Watch how other families work together and find good ones to emulate. It's amazing what can be learned just by watching and being aware, but anything can be improved with enough time and effort. Don't be afraid to ask questions; good parents rarely refuse to answer honest questions from people seeking help.

Testimony, obedience, charity, faith, and understanding, the same traits which help

> Champions do not become champions when they win the event, but in the hours, weeks, months and years they spend preparing for it. The victorious performance itself is merely the demonstration of their championship character.
>
> — Alan Armstrong

us return to our Heavenly Father, will help prepare us for Intentional Parenting and for raising the next generation of Intentional Parents. Like Nephi, parents working on these traits will be prepared to follow the guidance of the Spirit in all different circumstances.

A good example of teaching correct principles is Jacob, Nephi's brother. When his son Enos was ready and open to it, he remembered all that his father taught him. He had already prepared for this moment long before as a young man learning from his father:

> Behold, it came to pass that I, Enos, knowing my father that he was a just man—for he taught me in his language, and also in the nurture and admonition of the Lord—and blessed be the name of my God for it—
>
> And I will tell you of the wrestle which I had before God, before I received a remission of my sins.
>
> Behold, I went to hunt beasts in the forests; and the words which I had often heard my father speak concerning eternal life, and the joy of the saints, sunk deep into my heart.
>
> And my soul hungered; and I kneeled down before my Maker, and I cried unto him in mighty prayer and supplication for mine own soul. . . .[17]

Intentional Parents can have this same effect on their children even if it appears they're not listening. Later on at the right time, these children will remember what their parents taught them.

Whenever I feel like I finally have a handle on being a mother, something unexpected happens. Without fail, life is always changing which means new challenges, difficulties and concerns all the time. I wish I knew how complicated motherhood was before I had kids. I think I would prepare differently if I had known. I would try to prepare more for change: to look ahead, and know what's coming while praying for patience, faith, and guidance. Being a parent is the greatest—and the hardest—thing ever!

The story of the Army of Helaman is a favorite for most children. Their military success along with not one of them getting killed wasn't just a random coincidence. They were prepared with the faith necessary for this great responsibility by their parents who taught them and cared for them:

> Lucky parents who have fine children usually have lucky children who have fine parents.
> — James A. Brewer

Now they never had fought, yet they did not fear death; and they did think more upon the liberty of their fathers than they did upon their lives; yea, they had been taught by their mothers, that if they did not doubt, God would deliver them.

And they rehearsed unto me the words of their mothers, saying: We do not doubt our mothers knew it.

. . .

And now it came to pass in the second month of this year, there was brought unto us many provisions from the fathers of those my two thousand sons.[18]

Would it have been possible for them to be so greatly blessed without their parents teaching and guiding them? Probably not; they would not have been prepared and the outcome would most likely have been drastically different. Their parents prepared them to face life's challenges. Their fathers were providing and exemplifying while their mothers were nurturing and teaching them. We have been taught the same roles for mothers and fathers today in the *Family Proclamation*:

> By divine design, fathers are to preside over their families in love and righteousness and are responsible to provide the necessities of life and protection for their families. Mothers are primarily responsible for the nurture of their children. In these sacred responsibilities, fathers and mothers are obligated to help one another as equal partners.[19]

Every good character trait we want to see in our children, we need to work on ourselves. Prepare spiritually for hard times—times we all know will eventually come. Prepare physically as well. Whether this means building savings, acquiring food storage, getting out of debt, or something else entirely, as children watch their parents follow the prophets' counsel and work on these or other big tasks, they will see the importance their parents place on preparation. As they help their parents work towards these big goals, kids can learn what it takes to research, plan, and prepare for the future. These are valuable skills every child needs to learn for themselves and for their future families.

Whatever life hands out, whether it's building a ship or raising the next generation of Intentional Parents, preparation leads to more success with the challenges of life.

Goals,
All Shapes and Sizes

Imagine the struggle it would take to put together a one thousand piece puzzle without being allowed to see the picture on the box top first. The only thing visible would be a thousand tiny puzzle pieces. Starting with the edges might help, but it still gives very little guidance for which way is up or the measurements of each side and nothing of the picture itself. On the other hand, having the box top visible is extremely helpful. The picture guides our decisions for how to separate all the pieces of one pattern, gives us dimensions, and, most importantly, shows us the goal we're aiming for. Parenting can sometimes feel like doing a puzzle without the picture on the box top. On the other hand, having the picture on the box to help assemble the puzzle is an example of how Intentional Parenting works.

Perhaps a good way to describe what intentional means is this: there is always a big picture reason behind the actions of an Intentional Parent. Important actions are not decided on a whim, a certain mood, or as a reaction to something else. What we're talking about is much more than just deliberately choosing to become a parent. It's about choosing a parenting style in which the big picture or end goal is the deciding factor for all important decisions.

The key is deciding on the end goal and having it always clearly in mind.

What would be an end goal or big picture for parenting? If I want my kids to be independent and strong, it takes a different type of parenting than raising dependent children. End goals matter. Once we have a goal or big picture in mind, making a plan to get there is much easier. It reminds me of *Alice in Wonderland:*

"Cheshire-Puss," she began, rather timidly, as she did not at all know whether it would like the name: however, it only grinned a little wider.

"Would you tell me, please, which way I ought to go from here?"

"That depends a good deal on where you want to get to," said the Cat.

"I don't much care where---" said Alice.

"Then it doesn't matter which way you go," said the Cat.

"---So long as I get *somewhere,*" Alice added as an explanation.

"Oh you're sure to do that," said the Cat, "if you only walk long enough."[20]

If we don't care how our children grow up, the way we parent doesn't matter. But with a goal in mind, it's much easier to make a plan and know where we're going.

Of course, parenting isn't the only thing that counts. Among other things, agency and personality play a big part as well, but parents do have a huge role! Many just don't realize how big it really is. The more deliberate and purposeful a parent is in raising a child, the better effect that parent will have. Any style of parenting, good, bad, or just average, will have a big impact on a child. Great planning doesn't mean there won't be many surprises and unexpected events along the way, but Intentional Parents will almost always have better outcomes.

The best example of Intentional Parenting is our Heavenly Father since He is the Perfect Parent. One example of God's Intentional Parenting is His interaction with Nephi:

> . . . I have received a commandment of the Lord that I should make these plates, for the special purpose that there should be an account engraven of the ministry of my people.
>
> Upon the other plates should be engraven an account of the reign of the kings, and the wars and contentions of my people; wherefore these plates are for the more part of the ministry; and the other plates are for the more part of the reign of the kings and the wars and contentions of my people.
>
> Wherefore, the Lord hath commanded me to make these plates for a wise purpose in him, which purpose I know not.
>
> But the Lord knoweth all things from the beginning; wherefore, he prepareth a way to accomplish all his works among the children of men; for behold, he hath all power unto the fulfilling of all his words. And thus it is. Amen.[21]

The Lord knew He needed an alternate plan for the first 116 pages of the *Book of Mormon* translation. To accomplish this, He had Nephi make a second set of plates. The Lord was looking at the results or end goal He wanted more than 2000 years in the future, and that plan would shape how he interacted with Nephi. Because He deliberately asked Nephi for two sets of plates, we still have the first 450 years or so of the *Book of Mormon*.

Another example is how God sent Nephi and his brothers back for the Brass Plates. We learn how this actually gave them a way to teach their children to read and write as well as to teach them the gospel.[22] Having those plates made a big difference for Nephi's posterity. The Lord had a specific outcome He wanted and this colored the decisions made.

> Aim at heaven and get earth thrown in. Aim at earth and you get neither.
> — C. S. Lewis

Similarly, if parents have an end goal in mind, it's easier to make decisions concerning what would be good for the family and what wouldn't; what would be needed to accomplish those goals and what would be detrimental. So much confusion exists today about parenting. If we follow God's pattern of keeping the end goal in sight, we're bound to be more successful.

Surprisingly, choices we make usually have both good *and* bad consequences almost every time. This happens because of many short term and long term factors. An easy example would be eating potato chips, ice cream, or chocolate. At the time, it tastes delicious and having more tastes even better, but later on, it adds to those few nagging pounds to be lost. Another example is doing the dishes. I never want to do the dishes in the evening, but getting up in the morning to a sink full of dirty dishes to start the day is even worse. My choices are: do the dishes in the evening (not fun) and wake up to a clean kitchen (awesome) or leave the dishes (my evening is easier) and then have to tackle them in the morning (much less fun). Even more long term would be decisions like building up a savings account. Short term, it's not fun to tighten the budget and skip some things that might be fun for the family. Long term, we have savings for emergencies or a nice vacation—we all feel better about that. Family Night is another good example: when the children are fidgeting and teasing each other and won't sit quietly even for the thirty second lesson, it just doesn't seem worth it. But years down the road, when those same children are teens and understand the gospel principles within their own budding testimonies, it becomes obvious how very worth it all those crazy family nights were.

It's all in our perspective: if we only look at the short term consequences, the picture will always look strikingly different than if we see the long term consequences. But the trouble comes in how easy it is to ignore the long term consequences and focus on the short term as though that's all there is. Choices will often be dramatically different when the focus is on the long term.

When my kids were still very young, my husband started earning enough money that I felt we could afford to have someone come in and clean our house. I thought it was such a great idea because it would give me more time with my kids. It was working out great until my oldest daughter turned 13 and I realized she had never dusted or cleaned anything in her life. It finally dawned on me how this might affect her when she grew up and had her own home and family. I let the cleaners go on the spot and started teaching my kids to clean.

When children are involved, it only exaggerates—and complicates—the outcomes between short term and long term. Making a good decision is tough when tired, grouchy children are involved. (It's hard enough with only tired, grouchy parents.) It seems very simple to ignore the big picture when the short term is screaming for attention, but challenges and tough times are what make us strong.

Gathering our children around us and informing them of the decision to do some jobs together, maybe washing dishes or cleaning the car, will not go over extremely well to begin with. They might cry, complain, and throw tantrums and, honestly, it would be easier to just give up and tell them to forget it and go play. But that's the short term answer. The long term consequences of continuously letting them off the hook mean children who don't learn how to work, expect others to always do it for them, and never learn the value of working hard and its associated successes. If the long term wins, it means helping children learn, training them, and checking their work. (And sometimes listening to them complain.) The long term reward is children who can help; they can work and clean and watch younger siblings. The long term is great for how children will learn the value and commitment of work, but the short term sometimes feels just a bit like torture. Having gone through the short term myself and now seeing the long term, I think the "torture" was definitely worth it, but the hard part is being willing to go through with it even when the reward is so far in the future. I guess parents need discipline too—this is probably part of our Parenting 101.

> . . . By small and simple things are great things brought to pass. . . .
> — Alma 37:6

Planning and hard work are an important part of Intentional Parenting. As President Thomas S. Monson taught: "Wishing will *not* make it so. The Lord expects our thinking. He expects our action. He expects our labors. He expects our testimonies. He expects our devotion."[23] When Intentional Parents make goals for our families and work towards them with the big picture or long term goals in mind, the Lord will bless those efforts. In turn, our children will also be blessed.

President Kimball spoke about a personal goal he made when he was young and the lasting impression it made on him:

Let me tell you of one of the goals that I made when I was still but a lad. When I heard a Church leader from Salt Lake City tell us at conference that we should read the scriptures, and I recognized that I had never read the Bible, that very night at the conclusion of that very sermon I walked to my home a block away and climbed up in my little attic room in the top of the house and lighted a little coal-oil lamp that was on the little table, and I read the first chapters of Genesis. A year later I closed the Bible, having read every chapter in that big and glorious book.

I found that this Bible that I was reading had in it 66 books, and then I was nearly dissuaded when I found that it had in it 1,189 chapters, and then I also found that it had 1,519 pages. It was formidable, but I knew if others did it that I could do it.

I found that there were certain parts that were hard for a 14-year-old boy to understand. There were some pages that were not especially interesting to me, but when I had read the 66 books and 1,189 chapters and 1,519 pages, I had a glowing satisfaction that I had made a goal and that I had achieved it.

Now I am not telling you this story to boast; I am merely using this as an example to say that if I could do it by coal-oil light, you can do it by electric light. I have always been glad I read the Bible from cover to cover. . . .[24]

This story speaks of a family with Intentional Parents who planned, made goals, worked hard, and taught their children to do the same. Goals are an important part of progression. Children can feel the same satisfaction in accomplishing a goal adults can and it makes all the difference if they try. It's crucial for them to see their parents make goals and work to achieve them. It's a valuable example for them and it's even beneficial for them to see their parents work at a goal and fail. Seeing them make the attempt, even if it's not successful, is still effective. Children learn life doesn't always work as planned but they can still trust in God and not lose hope just like their parents.

Our Intentional Heavenly Father shows us these ultimate end goals when we study the Plan of Salvation. It's also why we learn about Adam and Eve and the Creation. Those truths help us see the big picture, the eternal consequences, which can be vastly different from the short term worldview. He gives us those examples to guide us as we intentionally make our choices.

Raise a Family
in the Lord

We are here, then, to be happy—each one of us—and to find real joy, but there is no real joy in this earth outside of fulfilling this great commandment of raising a family in the Lord. We are here to raise that family (not just raise a family, but raise a family *in the Lord*). That will take the very best that's in [us]. Yes, it will take sacrifice and it will take obedience. . . .[25]

Elder Hartman Rector Jr. said this as part of a talk in 1973 but I think it's even more relevant today. And besides the sacrifice and obedience he mentions, it will take a lot of patience, time, energy, love, prayer, faith, and inspiration; just to name a few. But all those are possible if we rely on Christ and teach our children to rely on Him as well. It is only with His help that we can successfully "raise a family in the Lord."[26] These attributes come as we grow, stretch, and faithfully parent our children; all the while teaching them to follow the same course with our precious grandchildren. Elder Douglas W. Shumway of the Seventy taught:

Loving, protecting, and nurturing our children are among the most sacred and eternally important things we will do. Worldly belongings will vanish, today's number-one movie or song will be irrelevant tomorrow, but a son or a daughter is eternal.[27]

What an awesome assignment we have been given to raise an eternal family! I know my husband and I can't possibly live up to that responsibility by ourselves. Without the Lord's help, I have no doubt we would fail.

Sometimes we hear half-joking complaints of children not coming with a direction manual, but they really do—God's version of a direction manual. We can get all the help we need if we're willing to pray, listen to the Spirit, and follow His counsel. Our Heavenly Father is the best source for help. He knows each of our children individually, in fact much better than we do, and He is willing to help us if we ask. Rather than deciding for ourselves what to do, or what's worse, just reacting in the moment, we can turn to the Lord for help. He will bless us with increased love, patience, understanding, or whatever it is we need at the time we need it most. Our children are also His children and He wants our families to succeed and return to Him.

One day my daughter came home very upset, her anger increasing with every passing moment. Very quickly she was beyond listening or calming down. As I watched her, I felt like I was looking at an angry cat, back arched, claws bared, and ready to strike. After trying to talk with her but getting nowhere, my first impression was to send her to her room until she calmed down. I hate to admit it but I did not want to deal with her temper right then. As I continued to watch her, I distinctly felt the inspiration to hug her. I'm embarrassed to admit it but this was the last thing I wanted to do so I ignored the prompting. Thankfully He didn't give up and I felt it again, "Hug her." Very reluctantly I reached out and put my arms around my daughter and, rather than feeling the claws digging in as I was expecting, she melted in my arms and her anger turned to tears.

Finally, I was able to break through that seemingly impenetrable shell and find out what was really bothering her. We were able to work everything out. If I hadn't followed that inspiration, this experience would have ended with her in her room where the issue would never have been resolved. Instead it ended in working through the problem with love and understanding that I really didn't think I was capable of right then. This experience was an eye opener for me. It really helped me realize how much God knows and cares about His children, and if I listen to the Spirit, even when it seems crazy, the results will always be better.

There are many instances when we may have no idea what to do. Those are times when perhaps only God has the answer and we can only find it through His help. If we come to Him humbly and prayerfully, we may be out of plans, patience, or good humor, but He will inspire us. He knows and loves our children and will help us raise them if we listen to His promptings. We shouldn't feel like we are alone in this sacred responsibility; He wants to help us raise His children.

My son was not healthy. Something was wrong and I wasn't figuring it out. I thought it might be allergies to foods, etc., but nothing was helping.

I was praying one night about him, asking for help, pondering about the issues he was having, when the Spirit prompted me to look up Celiac Disease. I didn't know much about it but as I looked it up, the Spirit confirmed to me that this is what he had: a very clear, direct answer!

When I went in to ask the doctor to test him, he told me I was just being a "mama bear" and he refused to test my son. We paid out of pocket to get the testing done and then took the very positive test results back to the GI doctor.

I am so thankful Heavenly Father leads us as parents and can give us answers that we may never come across on our own otherwise! He loves our kiddos and wants them to be healthy and happy too; we just need to remember to ask for help!

It is never an accident when children are raised correctly. Teaching them to follow God, recognize true principles, and understand His teachings rarely just happens. These are ideas that must be pondered, experienced, and internalized over time. Sending a child to church for a few hours each Sunday to learn these valuable lessons while living all week under a different standard won't bring the desired results. Nothing can take the place of good parents who understand their role, rely on God, and act accordingly every day.

Often in our culture we tend to recognize a problem, get frustrated thinking about it, and then just put it on the back burner. It's easier to ignore it rather than make a choice. Decisions are hard; many consequences are involved. If I choose path A, I automatically can't choose a number of other avenues, maybe B, C, or D, which would have different consequences. Slogging through this decision-making process explains why we procrastinate or even give up altogether. But this can give a false impression: if I don't actually make a decision, maybe I won't be responsible for what occurs. However, deciding not to decide is just as much a decision as choosing between alternatives. Even worse, I am leaving *everything* to chance instead of trying to make the best decision I can with God's help. Rather than choosing, I am allowing someone else to make the choice for me while I am no less

> And they shall also teach their children to pray, and to walk uprightly before the Lord.
> — D&C 68:28

responsible and the consequences will be just as real. My thinking through the decision, praying about it, talking it over with my spouse and others close to me, and then making the best choice I can with our eternal goals in mind is a far better course of action. Leaving things to chance rarely goes well; when we don't struggle through those decisions, we don't grow.

Another consequence of leaving our decisions to chance is that we aren't exhibiting the faith necessary for God's help. Intentional Parenting would be nearly impossible without His help. My family needs those blessings which mean faithful, purposeful decision-making can't be ignored. I want God's version of successful Intentional Parenting.

> Behold, it came to pass that I, Enos, knowing my father that he was a just man—for he taught me in his language, and also in the nurture and admonition of the Lord—and blessed be the name of my God for it—[28]

33

When I first read this, years ago, I thought Enos must have been the perfect child, but that's not necessarily true. He might have acted like he was not paying much attention at all as a teen. It may have taken years for it to sink in while his father could have felt like giving up numerous times. Our children may be that same way. Jacob, Enos' father, didn't give up and neither can we. When we really trust God and believe He will help us, we need to take that step of faith into the darkness where there is seemingly no heavenly help. Once He sees we are willing to do the work to follow Him, He will send His Spirit with inspiration and guidance, but first we have to take that step of faith on our own.

Intentional Parents put their children first. It takes a lot of time, effort, and patience to raise good children. If parenting is way down on the list of priorities, then it won't be intentional and it also probably won't be as successful. President Spencer W. Kimball warned us of allowing other interests to replace parenting:

Do not, however, make the mistake of being drawn off into secondary tasks which will cause the neglect of your eternal assignments such as giving birth to and rearing the spirit children of our Father in Heaven. Pray carefully over all your decisions.[29]

C. S. Lewis understood this same principle, "The homemaker has the ultimate career. All other careers exist for one purpose only—and that is to support the ultimate career."[30] Somehow we have turned it all backwards. Today, families are to support everything else rather than everything supporting our families. Imagine the difference if we could restore the home and the homemaker to their rightful place.

Intentional Parenting needs to be at the top of the priority list along with God and spouse. Knowing where our children are, who they're with, and what they're doing is part of Intentional Parenting. We should keep tabs on them and make our homes places where they want to gather. We have much more influence in our own homes than in someone else's.

We can also spend time with our children and show them they matter. One-on-one time is significant. Even just having one child help mom or dad with errands, doing dishes, or folding clothes can give parents that bit of time together with a child. Planning ahead can make a big difference; time together matters. Society emphasizes quality time but Intentional Parents need to understand the value of quantity time as well. Quality time cannot be forced, scheduled, or mandated; it's something that just happens and usually comes only after large amounts of quantity time have already taken place. There's no way to hurry this along:

> [Parents] must not fall into the trap of believing that "quality" time can replace "quantity" time. Quality is a direct function of quantity—and [parents], to nurture their children properly, must provide both.[31]

Quality time has to be fostered through quantity time. We need to be there when they need us there, not just when it's convenient: waiting up when they come home after a date or from a friend's house, being there after school as they walk in the door, watching their games and recitals many evenings or weekends, always being there when friends come over, and much more. The best time to

> In family relationships, love is really spelled T.I.M.E.
> — Dieter F. Uchtdorf

talk is when they are ready to talk; if we are giving them quantity time, we will be there for those moments of infrequent, spontaneous, quality time. So much can happen then! When one of those moments occurs, it's urgent we run with it. Now I'm not saying drop everything at the slightest hint of their engaging, but important questions, serious concerns, and their willingness make these times a priority.

Patience is another big part of parenting from the very beginning to the very end. At every turn our patience is tested. In fact, I've decided it's a child's job to test their parents as much as possible. If my patience is intact without much effort on my part, I assume someone must be up to something. I better find any missing kids because they are probably hiding somewhere planning all sorts of deviousness. As parents we pray to keep a calm demeanor and quiet voice, but we need to be willing to forgive ourselves for our own mistakes too. We try our best but moms and dads are imperfect too. In the end, we're all here to learn and improve, whether it's Parenting 101 or Stripling Warriors 101. When our children see us working on our own shortcomings, our example can help motivate them.

Intentional Parenting can be a very humbling experience. Something will occur almost daily which can leave us completely baffled. Just when I think things are going smoothly, something always happens to shake everything up again.

I thought I had pretty much figured out parenting when my 5th child was born. She would lie in my arms during sacrament meeting while my four older children reverently looked through books. That's when I made the mistake of thinking that I must be an exceptional mother. . . . Within the week, my sweet baby started crawling. From that moment on, she never held still and was never quiet. I found myself saying, "Holly, don't do that!" "Holly, be quiet," "Holly, stay here," and "Holly, get down off of the refrigerator!" I didn't know how to work with this child who didn't work with reason. She only worked with what she felt at the moment.

I prayed to know how I could help her, I had tried everything I knew and it just wasn't working. Almost immediately I received an answer, Holly needed to learn love and she couldn't if I expected her to act like her older siblings. From that point on, I made it a point to show her lots of love. She still needs correcting at times, but she has no doubt that we love her!

With microwaves and pre-packaged everything today, our instant gratification "gene" becomes impatient and we want to "zap" everything to work flawlessly. Since science and technology work by building on past knowledge, we sometimes think our children should come ready to do the same but human nature doesn't work that way. Every child starts at the beginning with their personal faith and knowledge of God's plan. It took slow, steady learning to get us where we are as parents and it will take the same for our children.

It's extremely important we don't assume our kids know something is true because we know it's true. Unless they have internalized a principle for themselves, they can't really have a testimony of it yet. They might obey us but that's not the same as having their own testimony. If they gain a testimony of these principles themselves, they will be stronger and much more faithful in their own right.

Teaching our children faith and prayer are the first steps in helping them look to God for their own guidance and inspiration. God can help them in ways we parents can't; that's what Intentional Parenting is all about: teaching our children to follow God on their own.

Another goal of Intentional Parenting is to prepare our children to raise their own children as future stripling warriors full of faith and resolve to follow God. Our work involves trying to improve the chances of success for the next generation and the one after that; I don't mean an improvement in money or material goods, but something more eternal: a strong faith and testimony with courage to remain faithful and return to God. Elder Richard L. Evans taught us how God did His intentional work:

> There seems to be little evidence that the Creator of the universe was ever in a hurry. Everywhere, on this bounteous and beautiful earth, and to the farthest reaches of the firmament, there is evidence of patient purpose and planning and working and waiting.[32]

I can't even imagine the depth of patience, sacrifice, and commitment in time and energy our Father in Heaven has given for our benefit. My own part as a parent pales in comparison and yet can still sometimes feel enormous to me. If I can bring to my home just a tiny spark of the

> Patience is a virtue that has to be learned. No one comes here with patience.
> — Hartman Rector Jr.

feeling captured here by Elder Evans, I know my Intentional Parenting will succeed because God will be by my side all the way. We really *can* raise our families in the Lord.

As a mother, I knew I would experience heartbreak, I just didn't know how that heartbreak would come. About eight months ago we learned that our son had an addiction to pornography. He had first been exposed to it at the age of eight and he continued to be lured to it. His addiction had escalated to the point where he was viewing pornography consistently for the past two years. He was actively engaged in finding ways to view it and how to hide it from us. Satan had him in a stranglehold and he later told us, "I honestly believed there was no way out." It was during one of his moments of struggle when we learned of his problem. So great was his struggle that for the first time in years he prayed for help, and to his relief help came. I awoke that same night with an urgency to check the house. The feeling that something wasn't right was so strong. That was the night I first encountered our son's pornography addiction. One week later we would learn the full extent of his struggle.

As parents we didn't know what we were facing. No words can adequately describe the anguish that we felt. It was in those first moments that our faith in Christ began to be tested. I will never forget holding my son in my arms as he cried, "I'm so glad you know. I want to stop but I can't do it by myself." My son had exercised the small amount of faith he had managed to hold onto to cry out to his loving Heavenly Father for help. Now it was up to us as his parents to use our faith to help rebuild his. In the days, weeks, and months that followed our family's desires and perspective became that of helping our son heal.

There is no way to adequately describe the anguish of a broken heart, but it was through that heartbreak that I saw glimpses of the divine. I saw first-hand the redemptive power of the atonement! I saw a loving Father in Heaven lead my husband and me ever so carefully. He guided our speech and our actions toward our fragile and broken son during those first vital months. I witnessed miracles, beautiful miracles! I know first-hand the wisdom in the council for mothers to stay in the home. If both my husband and I had to worry about an early morning job, who would be there on those hard nights our son continues to face? He needs me there to help bear him up. How grateful I am that he did not and does not face those nights alone!

I have often sat in wonder as I realized that it is through this hard trial that my love for my son grew in ways I never imagined. The love between son and father grew and the love between siblings grew. In short, our heartbreak is turning out to be beautiful.

I know that as my son continues to climb this mountain, there will be times when he will slip and fall. It will be during those times that I will be there to carry him. To hold him and remind him how much he is loved by his family and God. He isn't perfect, but our Savior Jesus Christ is and through him we may become perfect.

There may be many more heartbreaks; heartbreaks that come with this mortal experience, but I know that God loves me. I am a mother to His precious children. I know miracles happen! Most importantly, I have faith in my Heavenly Father and I know that He will guide me if I but choose to follow Him.

The Intricacies of Agency

I once heard a young wife, expecting her first child, comment on how she planned to teach her child about modesty, "I'm not going to take away my daughter's agency. I'm going to be a good example for my daughter by acting and dressing modestly and then I won't have to say anything to her; I just know she will follow my example and be modest too." That is an excellent goal! However I think most mothers who have experienced teen-aged daughters will admit it doesn't quite work that way. There is excessive pressure from media and friends teaching how immodesty is cool and beautiful. Going shopping and trying to find cute, modest clothes doesn't help much either. Immodest outfits are effortless to find while it takes searching to find modest, trendy fashions teens will love. All this causes most girls to dress immodestly to fit in. The good example from their mothers, whom they consider old anyway (sorry, Moms, but it's true), are not going to convince them to act and dress modestly when almost everyone their own age is doing just the opposite. Example is a crucial part of raising children, teaching one thing and doing another never works, but Intentional Parenting takes more than just example.

The fallacy of using example by itself becomes obvious when the same rule is applied to other things children do. Will children always brush their teeth—and do it consistently every night and morning following all the correct procedures—because they watch their parents do it? Will children always fasten their seatbelts in the car without any reminders simply because they watch their parents buckle up? Will parents never have to tell children no more sugary snacks because they should just notice their parents' healthy choices? Will parents never have to grab a wandering child out of the busy road because their example of staying on the sidewalk should be enough?

Most parents are comfortable setting rules for issues like hygiene, safety, and sugar. They naturally understand rules are necessary for this. Yet somehow this doesn't carry over to religious matters such as modesty, church attendance, or good media habits. These parents may say, "But it's about saving our children's lives when it comes to busy roads and seatbelts and it's about keeping them healthy when we're talking about snacks and brushing teeth."

That apparently makes it different than religious matters, but does it really? Is a child's spiritual health any less important than their physical health? If we think about what Christ taught; "Not that which goeth into the mouth defileth a man; but that which cometh out of the mouth, this defileth a man,"[33] children's spiritual well-being is just as vital—or even more so—than their physical well-being. Rules at home need to reflect that.

Setting these types of rules is usually where parents begin to worry about hurting a child's agency. The problem comes in how to find that line between taking away children's freedom altogether and allowing children to abuse their agency, others, and/or themselves. Neither extreme constitutes good parenting. Between them is a middle ground where parents can help children learn to use their agency to bless the world around them.

As part of our church teachings, we often hear the Creation story, and it's easy to wonder why. The Creation is the only connection we have to a place outside of this world. It draws us out of our normal personal experience and allows us to view the big picture of why we are here and what God's purpose is. Sometimes it's so easy to get caught in the minute details; we forget the overarching perspective our Heavenly Father has. That reminder is the key to thriving in this life and really understanding the importance of returning to our heavenly home. Our world is full of ways to help us forget there's anything more to living than having a good time. We all need reminders of that big picture over and over again.

Our Heavenly Father gave us all agency; it's part of our eternal natures and an essential part of God's plan for us, but agency never stands alone. To help us learn how to use our agency, the Lord, as part of His Plan of Salvation, established laws and their consequences. How we follow those laws shows whether we are choosing Christ or not. Their consequences, both good and bad, are to emphasize those laws and help motivate us towards better choices next time.

> Wherefore, men are free according to the flesh; and all things are given them which are expedient unto man. And they are free to choose liberty and eternal life, through the great Mediator of all men, or to choose captivity and death, according to the captivity and power of the devil; for he seeketh that all men might be miserable like unto himself.[34]

What a perfect pattern for parents to use as a model! Choices are permanently tied to consequences. But those everyday choices don't have just physical consequences; they have eternal consequences as well. Intentional Parents need to teach their children about the connection between choices they make and their consequences, both physical and eternal.

Alma explained this connection to his son Corianton:

> . . . How could he sin if there was no law? How could there be a law save there was a punishment?
>
> Now, there was a punishment affixed, and a just law given, which brought remorse of conscience unto man.
>
> Now, if there was no law given—if a man murdered he should die—would he be afraid he would die if he should murder?
>
> And also, if there was no law given against sin men would not be afraid to sin.[35]

God instituted laws with consequences giving us a path to follow. With those laws in place it's pretty hard to plead ignorance. While children may be too young to follow this path set by our Heavenly Father, He solved this problem by giving them parents. As parents search for correct principles to teach and guide their children, it enables children to learn what obedience and choosing correctly feels like. Homes should be small replicas of God's Plan. There are rules to follow and consequences in place for those rules. This helps children understand how God and His Plan of Salvation work. He leads and inspires us but follows through with the bad consequences when a choice is made which breaks His laws. As children grow up watching their parents' example and experiencing the rules and consequences their parents utilize, children also learn how God's Plan works.

A few days ago my 8-year-old was in trouble for not cleaning her room the day before. I told her if she didn't get her room clean she would be grounded all day. When my visiting teachers stopped by she was able to sneak downstairs to join her siblings. When I realized this, we had a little chat. I reminded her that she was grounded and told her if she chose to go back downstairs she would be grounded for another day but it was her choice. She stood in the kitchen and thought about it for a minute, almost started heading back downstairs but then decided to return to her room instead. I could have easily made her go back in her room, but I have found that she just repeats the same mistakes and then blames me because I "got her in trouble." I have learned that she needs to be allowed to make her own choices and to deal with the consequences. If I allow her to make her own choices, she learns better. I only give consequences I'm willing to follow through on. I give choices to my kids when they are young, choices I can live with like "You pick the pants, I pick the shirt," or "Do you want peas or corn for dinner?" It's still their choice but their options have been narrowed. It allows us to have a better relationship and teaches her that she can make choices but she can't always choose the consequences.

The scriptures promise, "Train up a child in the way he should go: and when he is old, he will not depart from it."[36] The most important word in that sentence is "train." Parents have been given the responsibility to train their children. A good definition of "train" comes from Webster's 1828 Dictionary. It's an older definition which varies somewhat from ours today, but it's closer to the original meaning of the words used when our scriptures were translated:

To draw along; to entice; to allure, . . . by artifice or stratagem, . . . by persuasion or promise. To exercise; to discipline. . . . To educate; to teach; to form by instruction or practice; to bring up.[37]

How do parents put this into action? President Spencer W. Kimball gave us some great examples in a General Conference talk about raising children. He spoke of the necessity of parents to intentionally guard their children against the evils of the world:

On a cold winter day most children set out for school warmly clothed. The soles of their shoes are thick, and they wear boots over them. They wear heavy coats, with scarves around their necks and mittens on their hands—all to protect them from the inclemency of the weather. But are these same children protected against the mistaken ideologies and ideas of other youth and the temptations of the day?

The skin diver wears a heavy rubber suit to protect his body from the cold, but are children protected by prayer and family unity and spiritual training to shield them from the cold, dark world in which they eat and drink and sleep and play?

The outdoor worker is protected against the elements by proper apparel, but how often are children fully protected by a life of family devotion, family love and respect, family understanding, proper training and discipline?[38]

46

President Kimball spoke of physical and spiritual training, discipline, and prayer as well as the importance of teaching truths to offset those "mistaken ideologies and . . . temptations of the day."[39] There are many ways to go about doing this but the church has some recommendations; those include family prayer, daily family scripture study, and especially Family Home Evening where parents teach the doctrines of the gospel and share their testimonies. FHE is such an important time when parents can pinpoint each child's needs and address them right as they're occurring to help minimize any ill effects. There isn't a one-size-fits-all answer which is right for every family. Intentional Parents need to pray

> You have agency, and you are free to choose. But there is actually no free agency. Agency has its price. You have to pay the consequences of your choices.
> — Dieter F. Uchtdorf

and search out what will work for their children. Heavenly Father wants parents to succeed; He didn't leave us by ourselves to fail miserably. He will help us if we ask in faith and show Him we're serious about following Him and His prophets. The promises are there for our success; we just have to claim them.

Imagine life as a house with Christ as the foundation. We use our agency to design rooms and decorate the walls creating the actual house itself. But between designing and actually creating our house is an important step that must be followed: on our foundation we first have to build the frame for the house. This represents both God's laws and parents' rules. Without this framework, our walls won't stay up. We are free to design our house however we like with one rule: the walls have to fit the framework which has been built on the foundation. The frame is an essential component just like the foundation. Without it, we won't have any way to attach our walls no matter how beautifully they are designed.

Parents neglect this key framework when they choose to forego boundaries or rules; instead opting for their children to "use their agency" and decide for themselves. This leaves children with no frame or structure on which to anchor their choices. Not setting rules for a child is like telling them there are no right or wrong answers as far as their parents are concerned. Not giving them rules to follow with consequences is setting them up for failure. How can they learn what to do when there are no rules? It's important for children to not only see parents living the gospel principles but also to understand the significance placed on those principles. They can learn to not play in the road through a parent's explanation, but they will really understand the gravity of it by how quickly Dad goes after them and brings them back to safety. Children realize the value of sacred matters as parents emphasize their importance through their family rules.

My teenager was giving us such a hard time. She didn't want to go to seminary and kept trying to find ways to get out of it. Finally I sat her down one day and explained how I am responsible to God to do the best I can to raise her. I'm not perfect but I'm doing my best to listen to the Lord in raising my children. This is why she has to attend seminary. I think she finally understood. This didn't stop all the disagreements or make everything perfect, but it did help her understand it from my point of view and after that she seemed a bit more willing to obey.

Children are continuously bombarded with worldly messages which can lead them down wrong paths. Consequently they need constant reinforcement from God's side through church and especially their family. Children should be taught how to correctly use their agency just like they must be taught how to make their beds, share their toys, or play a musical instrument. Parents set rules and teach their children to follow them, and as children progress and get older, they will learn to govern themselves. If parents start when children are young, they will grow up already knowing and understanding these principles. They will still have trials and temptations, but they will be much better prepared to deal with them.

Habits help with things like hygiene but also with gospel standards. A girl who has always dressed modestly since she was little will already be in that habit later on when it really matters. Temptations will still come, but modesty has become part of her testimony. A boy who grew up in a home where they attended church regularly is forming a habit which can lead to growth in his testimony and strength when trials come. Strong personal testimonies in youth keep them on track when parents are not around as much anymore. The pressure from the other side is so great it is nearly impossible to follow God without a strong personal testimony.

My son wanted to play a videogame and my husband and I were conflicted about whether to allow him to play it or not. I did not feel the game was appropriate for our son. I could have just told him no but then he would resent me and always wonder why or he might sneak to play it at a friend's house or when I wasn't watching. The next morning my son and I sat down and talked about the game. I told him I was going to allow him to choose and I would respect his decision but I wanted to discuss it with him first. We pulled out the 13th Article of Faith and read through it then started looking at the game. As we talked about our standards and the video game, he started to cry because he realized that even though he desperately wanted to play the game, he shouldn't. He has never asked to play the game again. Allowing him to make his own choices and being willing to respect those choices has made a huge difference in our relationship.

In many ways our children are constantly being pulled in the direction of evil. We need to ensure they receive training from the good side to counteract the bad. So much time can be spent on worldly pursuits; perhaps that is why many recent prophets have been unwavering about the significance of doing the little things daily like reading scriptures and having family prayer. Giving children some time every day to remind them of the Savior and the real meaning of why they're here is vital. Just those small interruptions in the normal happenings of the day can refocus their minds, help them feel the Spirit, and remind them of heavenly things in the middle of all this earthly chaos.

President Kimball ended his talk with this warning:

How sad if the Lord should charge any of us parents with having failed to teach our children. Truly a tremendous responsibility falls upon a couple when they bring children into the world. Not only food, clothes, and shelter are required of them, but loving, kindly disciplining, teaching, and training. . . .

Home life, home teaching, parental guidance, father in leadership—these are the panacea for the ailments of the world, a cure for spiritual and emotional diseases, a remedy for problems. Parents should therefore not leave the training of children to [others]. The father and the mother must undertake this great responsibility, using the Church programs to assist them. Herein is the success the Lord wants to be achieved in the family home evening which He has established.

God is our Father. He loves us. He spends much energy trying to train us, and we should follow His example and love intensely our own children and rear them in righteousness. The parents who give their children their own way will fail, and so we must plan and organize our home life and bring our children up to be followers of the Lord Jesus Christ.[40]

Intentional Parents can follow his counsel and teach their children to do it too!

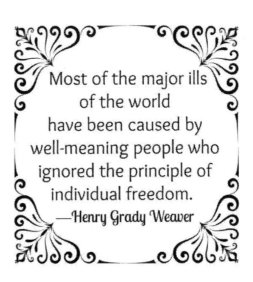

Most of the major ills
of the world
have been caused by
well-meaning people who
ignored the principle of
individual freedom.
—Henry Grady Weaver

Teaching Moments, Temporal and Eternal

You and I are here upon the earth to prepare for eternity, to learn how to learn, to learn things that are temporally important and eternally essential, and to assist others in learning wisdom and truth.[41] Understanding who we are, where we came from, and why we are upon the earth places upon each of us a great responsibility both to learn how to learn and to learn to love learning.

. . . Learning to love learning equips us for an ever-changing and unpredictable future. Knowing how to learn prepares us to discern and act upon opportunities that others may not readily recognize.[42]

In this quote, Elder David A. Bednar mentions three important aspects of education we don't often hear: "learn how to learn," "learn to love learning," and temporal knowledge is important but eternal knowledge is essential. These ideas are vital for educating the next generation of Intentional Parents. The first two ideas he mentions, loving to learn and learning how to learn, are important skills for successfully navigating through life. Once we understand them, it's much easier to learn those new ever-changing technologies, reach new career goals and standards, or work through any other curveball life sends us. These skills can help our children be more self-reliant and ready to face the world we live in. If we want our children to master these important abilities, we must work on them as well and intentionally share that curiosity and love with our children.

Elder Bednar's final point is a twist on what we term education today, and yet is really more accurate. Helping our children gain significant temporal education is an important part of Intentional Parenting: education that helps a child learn how to recognize true principles, navigate through life, and meet great people of the past and present who can be good role models. Dates, names, places, and other information, though important, do not compare to understanding past events and their effects on civilization. As our children gain this important temporal education, they can begin to apply their essential eternal education to understand it from a gospel perspective. When they do this, their understanding will increase dramatically.

> Fairy tales are more than true: not because they tell us that dragons exist, but because they tell us that dragons can be beaten.
> — G. K. Chesterton

There can be little worry of a child being too educated; the real problems are too little education, the wrong kind of education, or educating at the wrong time. If our dependence on our Heavenly Father for parenting help is a top priority, we will be guided in what is needed and when it is needful. Elder Robert D. Hales gives us a deeper understanding of those eternal essentials, such as faith, which we need to teach our children:

I join with faithful parents everywhere in declaring that we know who we are, we understand our responsibilities as parents, and we do not fear the wrath of the prince of darkness. We trust in the light of the Lord.

Like [Moses' mother] Jochebed, we raise our families in a wicked and hostile world—a world as dangerous as the courts of Egypt ruled by Pharaoh. But, like Jochebed, we also weave around our children a protective basket—a vessel called "the family"—and guide them to safe places where our teachings can be reinforced in the home and at church.

Ultimately, we guide them to the greatest of all houses of learning—the holy temple. . . .

As parents, we have the responsibility to help our children to "liken all scriptures [indeed, every part of the gospel of Jesus Christ] unto us [and unto our children] . . . for [the] profit and learning [of our families]."

Are we likening all of our children's gospel experiences to the real needs in their lives? Are we teaching them about the gift of the Holy Ghost, repentance, the Atonement, the sacrament, and the blessing of sacrament meeting as they meet the challenges in their lives? There is not enough time in formal meetings to teach our children everything they need to know. Therefore, we must take advantage of everyday teaching moments.

These moments are priceless. They come when we are working, playing, and struggling together. When they come, the Spirit of the Lord can help us know what to say and help our children accept our teaching. [43]

There really are great teaching moments in our homes everyday where we can discuss both temporal and eternal principles. At first it might be hard to recognize them, but they are there. The more practice we get in finding them, the more such moments we will notice.

I find if I stay up until my teens get home after being out with friends, it often ends up being the perfect time to talk with them about their social life, problems with friends, or things that happened which made them uncomfortable. Waiting until the next morning seems to dampen their enthusiasm to talk. I don't know if it's because they forget about it, it doesn't bother them so much anymore, or they find excuses for what happened, but they are not as willing to talk about it later on. Maybe it's because it's quiet at night and no one else is around. I don't know, but whatever it is, it's when they open up.

Not only do they want to talk through their experiences, they are also willing to listen more. It's hard because it's late and I'm usually tired, but if that's when they want to talk, I'll listen. I'm willing to take any opportunity, no matter how inconvenient, to praise their good actions, discuss better choices, or clear up gospel concerns which friends or others might have muddied up. I've come to the conclusion that always staying up till my kids get home is essential.

Everyone's temporal education should include all the basics. When deciding what to study past that, the Spirit is the best resource. We are all born with an assignment from God to accomplish. Following the Spirit's promptings in what to learn and how to learn it is crucial in being prepared to accomplish it. Parents as well as the children themselves can receive inspiration about their education:

My son came to me one summer when he was 15 or 16 and told me that he really wanted to learn more about socialism and communism. He heard me, my husband, and our older children talking about it but didn't really understand it as much as he would like. That year he probably read 10 to 12 books on the subject. Soon he was an expert, understanding much more than most people. Later he was called on a mission to a Russian-speaking former Soviet-bloc country. As he read his mission call, I knew he had been listening to the Spirit when he told me he needed to learn about socialism. I also knew he wouldn't be pulled into that system or be confused as to what was right or wrong. He understood why people are drawn to it and the problems and consequences of it. His education made a big difference with his mission and I believe it will continue to play a role in the rest of his life as well.

Our children might be young and nowhere near mission age, but that's the perfect time to prepare them to listen to the Spirit and discover the fun of learning. The scriptures ought to be one of our main sources for teaching our children. Lehi used the Brass Plates for that very purpose:

For it were not possible that our father, Lehi, could have remembered all these things, to have taught them to his children, except it were for the help of these plates; for he having been taught in the language of the Egyptians therefore he could read these engravings, and teach them to his children, that thereby they could teach them to their children, and so fulfilling the commandments of God, even down to this present time.[44]

Notice how long-range Lehi's plans reached. They extended all the way to his grandchildren—that's great Intentional Parenting!

Every part of our society is kept separate and distinct; this part is religion, that part is education, this part is recreation, etc. I don't think this is what God intended:

And thou shalt teach [these words] diligently unto thy children, and shalt talk of them when thou sittest in thine house, and when thou walkest by the way, and when thou liest down, and when thou risest up.[45]

Our faith should be front and center in every aspect of our lives including education, and our children need to see it. Family Home Evening and family scripture study are great places to begin using these teaching moments. While our children are still young, we can emphasize the principles of the gospel with scripture stories and family history stories. As our children mature and begin to understand the world's beliefs, we can relate what is happening in the world to doctrines of the gospel and help them discover eternal answers. This essential eternal education creates their spiritual foundation, but it will need much study and faith to have the strength to withstand the world's blows.

If we are to be better prepared as parents to use Elder Bednar's ideas, we also need to learn about our children's friends, their interests, their schools and educational system, and other things which affect their lives. We can't afford to completely delegate our children's important temporal education to others. They can help, but we always need to stay informed of what our children are learning and how they are progressing. In this day and age, we can never assume others will include essential eternal principles like we would when teaching our kids. We need to keep informed and stay aware. No one else cares for our children like we do; similarly, we can't expect them to teach like we would.

In this age of the internet, we really can learn any topic, it's all there. The problem is there's also a lot of junk out there too. It's really about figuring out how to maneuver through the garbage to find the important truths. That is the hard part but it's also the necessary part. Good information is only the beginning of what an important temporal education needs.

We should also keep abreast of current events and discuss these with our children before their opinions have already been formed. If they hear our faith-based views first,

> Educating the mind without educating the heart is no education at all.
>
> — Aristotle

it may prepare them for when they hear other more worldly opinions later on. Talking to our kids before they become too invested in other ideas gives us a chance to help them see God's way and not be drawn in by the world so easily. This can even be a family night project: study what the prophets have said and discuss it together. It will help make their teachings more meaningful and give us the opportunity to share our convictions with our children. As they see us search for gospel-centered answers, study them, and learn truths, they will see this as a pattern to follow. Our family's essential eternal education will continue moving along. When our children work at something until they figure it out, they will own it. If they work hard at their education, eternal and temporal, it will be theirs and they won't squander it. This same promise holds true for us as well.

It might take some time, but it's important to familiarize ourselves with the books and magazines our children are reading and the movies they're watching. Don't trust media to teach good principles. All types of media, including educational ones, are filled with many politically correct ideas at odds with church doctrine. Often they convey subliminal messages kids won't even realize they're absorbing. Pointing these out and how they differ from our faith is crucial even if the older ones roll their eyes at us. Our children's awareness of these messages will help keep them more immune. Once they begin believing these worldly ideas, it will be harder to teach them true gospel principles.

My son was walking home from church with some friends one Sunday when one of the girls brought up abortion and women's rights. My son was thrilled to later relate to me how he respectfully told her abortion was wrong and why. He really had been listening during our family discussions! Sometimes I wondered if he heard anything we said. You just never know with kids. . . .

Questions are a great way to get creative energy flowing in our children and teach without appearing to. Questions can also help start conversations. This shows our kids we're interested in them and care about their opinions. Ask a lot of questions and then assist them in finding eternal answers. This can help them learn how to learn and eventually love it. Were the consequences good? Did they make good choices? Did they understand where their actions would lead? Did it further society in a positive way? Did it add to, or take away from, our liberties? Did they have an achievable, good goal in mind? How did those actions affect future generations? What moral or principle can we learn from this? Once we learn this, can we relate it to our day and circumstances? Human nature doesn't change which means consequences will probably be similar today: what were those consequences? Do we want to experiment or just trust God when He said He never changes? What eternal principles can be learned? What temporal principles can be learned?

As we discuss questions like these with our children, we need to listen as well. When we really listen to understand their point of view, they may be more willing to listen to us. But we must really, truly listen with the intent to understand and not merely to respond.

I remember clearly the point where I realized that what I thought was a good conversation with one of my boys really wasn't. I began to see I was doing all the talking and he was doing all the listening. I felt a strong impression to just stop talking. When I finally did, he would open up and talk, but if I began to ask too many questions or comment too often, he would close down again. I literally had to stop talking if I wanted him to talk. Once I really began to listen, I learned so much more about what was happening in his life than he ever told me before. It was amazing the things he would tell me when I gave him a real opportunity. It didn't matter what I thought was listening, it had to be what he thought was listening. Once I figured that out, it made all the difference.

Their participation also helps foster more personal learning. As they respond with ideas and thoughts, the Spirit can touch their hearts and teach them. This is the best form of education. We should make every effort to experience this for ourselves and help our children do the same.

As Intentional Parents, we need to show our children our resolve to stay on the Lord's side. When we read, study, research, and ask questions, we will find the right temporal and eternal answers for ourselves; then we can help our children do the same and the Spirit will be right there inspiring and guiding.

The glory of God is intelligence, or, in other words, light and truth.

. . . I have commanded you to bring up your children in light and truth.

But verily I say unto you, my servant Frederick G. Williams, you have continued under this condemnation;

You have not taught your children light and truth, according to the commandments; and that wicked one hath power, as yet, over you, and this is the cause of your affliction.

And now a commandment I give unto you—if you will be delivered you shall set in order your own house, for there are many things that are not right in your house.[46]

> Listen earnestly to anything your children want to tell you, no matter what. If you don't listen eagerly to the little stuff when they are little, they won't tell you the big stuff when they are big, because to them all of it has always been big stuff.
> — Catherine M. Wallace

Brother Williams neglected to teach his children and was held accountable for this even though he was trying to follow God and further the gospel. He was one of Joseph Smith's counselors and very busy, I'm sure. But the Lord told him this was no excuse for neglecting to teach his children the eternal essentials. Similarly, our children are our most important work; they cannot be neglected for other pursuits and we as parents not be held responsible.

For Intentional Parents, the gospel must be the foundation of all we teach and also the measuring stick by how we judge all other topics. Our children need to see us often use gospel principles and teachings as the way to distinguish truth from falsehood. As they see our convictions measure the truth of various topics, it will strengthen them to do the same.

Facilitating our children's education, both important temporal education and essential eternal education, is a vital aspect of Intentional Parenting. Helping our children be aware of the world around them and how it relates to and affects their faith and family is important. Raising a generation to be better prepared than we were to lead the way for another future generation is the goal. Education, like Elder Bednar and Elder Hales describe it, can be one more link in helping our children progress on their journey towards becoming Intentional Parents.

Since it is so likely that children will meet cruel enemies, let them at least have heard of brave knights and heroic courage.

—C.S. Lewis

Discipline for Future Disciples

We may often be reluctant to share our own discipline stories, even positive ones. Sometimes it works better to hear it from a bystander and get their reaction as well:

I used to be a store manager for Blockbuster. One day this mother and son were checking out and the kid [yelled], "I want a candy bar. Wah wah." The mother keeps saying "No, I already told you no." Then this kid thinks he has a fool proof plan. The kid open[s] a Snickers bar right there and takes a bite. He then says "Now you have to buy it." The mother is shocked and says "You're absolutely right." Turns to me and says, "We'll have the candy bar also." I scan the candy bar and she says "Now, throw it away please."

The look on the kid's face was priceless.[47]

I was standing in line at a major supermarket and in front of me was a woman and a small girl (about [age] 4), and in front of them was a young mother, with a small boy (about [age] 3). The little boy asked his mother for a candy bar, and was told

"No." The little boy then asked for a candy bar again, and he was told "No" again. So at this point he decided to have a temper tantrum. He threw himself on the ground, cried, screamed, [and] called his mother a "stupid head," amongst all of the classic tantrum behavior. His mother then whispered to the mother standing behind her and they smiled, all while this little boy was hysterical about being denied a candy bar. His mother then took a candy bar from the shelf and put it in her cart. The boy was happy upon witnessing this and his tantrum stopped.

The mother and son then went through the checkout and paid. The mother then turned around and handed the candy bar to the little girl behind her in line. She looked directly at her son and said "Children who behave are rewarded, and children who throw tantrums and embarrass their mothers get nothing." She turned around on her heels and walked away from the boy who was left silent with his jaw . . . on the floor. . . . It was brilliant.[48]

Discipline, a word which often brings a lot of anxiety, fear, and misunderstanding, is a very difficult subject to discuss in this day and age of political correctness and worry of what others might think. Fear of government intrusion is also a cause of concern for parents. There are just too many stories of children being taken from their parents because they were disciplined in a way a neighbor or social worker disagreed with. Consequently, it is a subject that is often ignored or only joked about before quickly changing the subject. In fact, it is so seldom discussed we are losing the very idea of discipline and just how important it is. But the problem is children need discipline and correction.

No worries though, it is not my intent to tell any parent how to discipline or punish their children. That is a right reserved to the parents and should be between them, their children, and God. If children are to truly learn and progress towards adulthood, discipline will need to be tailored to fit the specific needs of each child. The goal here is to bring discipline back out into the open, explain it, define it, and give parents the knowledge they need to incorporate effective discipline into their parenting. But most of all, the goal is to help their children grow up into amazing adults ready for the challenges of life and their own parenting.

When we think of discipline today, we think of spanking, time outs, or other forms of punishment. But discipline and punishment are not synonymous terms though both are necessary in raising our future Intentional Parents. The definition of punishment in the 1828 Dictionary is very insightful:

The *punishment* of the faults and offenses of children by the parent, is by virtue of the right of government with which the parent is invested by God himself. This species of *punishment* is chastisement or correction.[49]

How interesting that in 1828 they recognized parental authority comes from God and its purpose is to correct a child.

Discipline, on the other hand, means much more than just punishing bad behavior. The 1828 Dictionary (Yup, I love this dictionary!) defines discipline this way:

To instruct or educate; to inform the mind; to prepare by instructing in correct principles and habits; as, to *discipline* youth for a profession, or for

67

future usefulness. . . . To instruct and govern; to teach rules and practice, and accustom to order. . . . To correct; to chastise; to punish.[50]

Discipline includes punishment but adds much more. Preparing and teaching through instruction can be very different from punishment, but both are part of discipline. Sometimes basic punishment is necessary, but often we can teach children, train them, and help prepare them to become adults with other methods that are more positive.

Discipline comes in many forms, but there are two over-arching types: negative and positive. Negative, in this sense, doesn't mean bad. It refers to taking away, removing something, or stopping bad behavior. Examples of negative discipline are spanking, grounding, time-out, and taking away privileges. Positive forms of discipline, on the other hand, refer to reinforcing the good behavior and include compliments, giving privileges, rewards, or even bribery.

Both negative and positive forms of discipline contain good and bad methods; it's up to us as parents to choose. Sometimes children are inspired to do better with compliments—being told they did a good job or how proud we are of them—and other times it doesn't work. It can take trying many different approaches to find what works with each child. It's not easy but the important part is not giving up even when it's challenging.

> Verily, thus saith the Lord unto you whom I love, and whom I love I also chasten that their sins may be forgiven, for with the chastisement I prepare a way for their deliverance in all things out of temptation, and I have loved you.
> — D&C 95:1

The first step is to follow the pattern set by our Heavenly Father. He established ground rules with consequences if they are not followed:

> Now . . . How could he sin if there was no law? How could there be a law save there was a punishment?
>
> Now, there was a punishment affixed, and a just law given, which brought remorse of conscience unto man.[51]

Our Father in Heaven established consequences for breaking His laws to help teach us, His children. A big part of discipline should be allowing children to experience the consequences of their actions. We can't fix everything for them or take away all consequences and still expect them to learn from their mistakes. We can give them ideas and even help them, but it's important to let them work it out themselves as much as they can. We cannot do it for them, but we can stand by them, help them, and guide them.

Now I'm not saying allow a child to be hit by a car as a consequence for running into the road. Before they were allowed to play outside, they should have been warned not to go into the road and what the consequence of disobeying would be. Maybe they were warned the consequences would be remaining inside while everyone else plays outside. Whatever it may be, the consequence needs to be imposed as soon as the rule is broken. All rules need a consequence which fits each child and their actions.

I had to write reports based on whatever I did wrong. Once I got caught in a lie and I had to write a report about 5 famous liars. Once I refused to take a bath and I had to write a report about germs. This was before the internet. We had a set of encyclopedias and that was it. It was surprisingly effective.[52]

I got caught skipping school when I was 14. My Dad told me that he was taking me out of school the next week. Every day that week he would drop me off at a local business (he knew all of these people) and told them "Here's your free helper! He doesn't want to go to school, so he gets to work!" They would work me, doing the worst [jobs] ever, for 8 hard hours every day.
One week of that and I was begging to go back to school.[53]

When we tell a child there will be a certain punishment for a certain action, we need to follow through with it. Empty threats won't work very long and they also disassociate punishments from actions. Following through with consequences may seem hard or inconvenient at the time, and often kids will try to make parents feel guilty, but following through will make a parent's job much easier in the end. If children know punishments always follow incorrect actions, they will soon learn those actions are not worth doing. Over time, the need for punishment often diminishes leaving other types of discipline, instruction and training, with a bigger role. This makes for a much calmer, happier home. We can also help our children understand this is how God works with us as well. This will help prepare them, knowing what He expects from them as well.

The events surrounding Joseph Smith and the beginning of the church show some insights into God's parenting style. Moroni, visiting Joseph in his bedroom a few years after the First Vision, repeated his message four times. God understands we need to hear things many times in order to remember them; our kids need repetition as well! The Lord had Joseph Smith come back to the Hill Cumorah once every year for four years to learn from Moroni. Why not teach him all at once, once a week, or even a little every day? Perhaps at least part of the reason was to teach him discipline and patience while allowing him to grow and mature and really internalize the message. Growth and maturity come as we teach. A small amount over time works better than all at once. Another time the Lord finally allowed to Joseph Smith to give Martin Harris the manuscript after repeated pleas. Once Martin lost them, the Lord then allowed Joseph to live with the consequences of his actions. He lost the right to translate for some time while he repented. Our Heavenly Father knows when we're not willing to listen we often must learn for ourselves by experiencing the consequences for our incorrect decisions.

These sorts of experiences helped Joseph grow and mature He learned to listen to God and obediently follow His guidance. I'm sure this helped him become the great prophet and leader he was. After experiencing consequences resulting from wrong choices, Joseph excelled in his prophetic role. Even though it's hard for us as parents to watch, our children will benefit from their hard experiences as well.

While the same method never works for every child or even the same child every time, it's amazing how some creativity and determination can make a huge difference:

My darling daughter, when she was six or seven, had a hard time transitioning from playing to anything else. If I told her we needed to go grocery shopping, or run an errand, she would get angry and yell that she wasn't going. It would quickly become a power struggle which never ended well. By that point, there was nothing I could do to calm her down and get her to behave. This got old really

71

fast. Trying to come up with different ideas, I decided to attempt some reverse psychology. The next time I needed to take my kids with me, I told them we were all going but not this daughter; she couldn't come. I would only take all the other kids. When I said that, she jumped up and said, "No, I'm coming! I want to go!" It worked! And not just once. This is how we learned to handle things for a couple years until she grew out of this phase.

A generation ago parents emphasized punishment much more. Today's parenting style is not just moving away from punishment but also from all kinds of discipline. Many parents want to be friends with their children. They want to believe their children will willingly obey because of their "friendship." But kids already have friends; what they need are parents acting with love and discipline. The Lord used discipline; that's why we call His followers disciples, not friends.

Some type of discipline is necessary to help a child see the importance of making good choices. Without consequences tied to actions, children will choose what seems the most popular or gives instant gratification over a better choice with long-term benefits. Intentional Parents can see roadblocks up ahead better than children and, through love and discipline, they can instruct and prepare them to make good choices which lead to positive long-term outcomes.

One day my little five-year-old boy came home after playing at our neighbors' with a new word in his vocabulary, a swear word. Needless to say, his mom and I were not pleased. We got angry and told him not to say it again but he did. Over the next few weeks we tried reasoning with him, bribing him, time-out, grounding, and, yes, even spanking him, besides just about everything else we could think of, but nothing seemed to help. One day the Bishop came for a visit and, of course, our son was still swearing. We didn't know what to do; we had already tried everything but he just kept swearing more and more. Our wise Bishop realized what we thought was punishment was actually reinforcing our son's bad behavior rather than stopping it like we hoped. What works really depends on each child because everyone is different. He could see that our son actually liked all the attention he was getting. The Bishop recommended we try a new tactic. Every time our son swore, we were to completely ignore him and give him no attention whatsoever. And when he didn't swear, we gave him a lot of attention. It took only a few days before he completely stopped swearing.

Creativity works; what doesn't work is when parents say, "Kids have their agency. They need to decide for themselves." And then proceed to give no consequences whatsoever. This is how many children are being raised today and it leaves them completely on their own to make important decisions without understanding or guidance in choosing wisely. This is not parenting. Our role as parents is to train and teach while trying our best to help our children grow in faith with a good understanding of gospel principles.

> Train up a child in the way he should go: and when he is old, he will not depart from it.
> — Proverbs 22:6

We need to reinforce good behavior and discipline bad behavior. If kids still make wrong choices, that is their decision; but if we as parents don't do our part, then we are left with much of the blame as well. Peer pressure and other worldly pressures will teach our children if we don't. These never stop or even slow down and the results are often not the best.

> One Christmas eve, I played sick while the family went to [church]. As soon as they left, I unwrapped all my presents and wrapped them back up very carefully. My mom didn't say a word when she came home and looked at the tree.
> The next morning, my favorite gift was nowhere to be seen, and my sister got a bunch of my clothes. I couldn't say anything.
> The next year (having decided I would just be more careful) I started unwrapping . . . each time [a present] was [placed] under the tree. They contained dead flowers and rocks taped to the box. Again, I couldn't even say anything.
> Mom told me years later she always knew when I was at it as I would stomp around the house and glare at everyone all day.[54]

Self-discipline is seldom something people are naturally born with. Usually it is learned through practice and teaching. Our job as parents is to instill this inner discipline in our children which can be there even for the difficult times, especially when parents are not around. Discipline is involved in athletics, art, music, dance, or most any other activity. We can utilize these to help instill self-discipline while we help our children master their talents.

As a child's inner discipline grows stronger with age and maturity, Intentional Parents will see this and can then gradually, over the years, relax their discipline but always remain vigilant. Everyone can acquire self-discipline; it just takes time and effort. It's why parents choose to vacuum, wash dishes, or take care of the yard when they would much rather be relaxing. We are disciplining ourselves. It's a good example for our kids to see. This is the goal in disciplining children: to help them arrive at the point where they can discipline themselves and follow God's plan for them.

My son came to me one Saturday when he was around 14 years old. He told me his friends got to choose whether they went to church or not. He wanted the same privilege from us. I thought about this a few minutes and told him I would let him choose when I thought he was old enough to make a good decision. He, of course, wanted that time to be right then. I asked him, "What would your decision be if I let you choose now?"

"I think I would sleep in and not go this week."

It didn't take me long to decide, "Well, that shows me you're not old enough to make the decision on your own yet. Make sure you're ready for church on time tomorrow."

In my mind, being old enough to make the decision meant making the right decision and my son knew it.

Peer pressure and worldly interests will always be there to push and prod our children. If these are unopposed, they usually win. Children are potentially exposed to hours and hours each week of detrimental experiences which could harm them spiritually as well as mentally or physically. School, friends, and all kinds of media can— and often do—have a bad influence on children. Taking them to church for a few hours on Sunday, even with a couple hours during the week for activities, is just not enough to counter the harmful messages they are constantly receiving. They need more positive spiritual influences. In fact, we parents do as well. All of us can work together on this and grow in strength to stand against anything the adversary might throw at us. That's why our church leaders have asked us to have daily scripture study and family prayers, weekly family nights, and always maintain open communication with our children. These seem like such minor things but they really are a big deal. Children will not have the strength to withstand the onslaught of opposition if they have not been given the tools to do so. The armor of God is real and our kids need it:

Put on the whole armour of God, that ye may be able to stand against the wiles of the devil.

For we wrestle not against flesh and blood, but against principalities, against powers, against the rulers of the darkness of this world, against spiritual wickedness in high places.

Wherefore take unto you the whole armour of God, that ye may be able to withstand in the evil day, and having done all, to stand.

Stand therefore, having your loins girt about with truth, and having on the breastplate of righteousness;

And your feet shod with the preparation of the gospel of peace;

Above all, taking the shield of faith, wherewith ye shall be able to quench all the fiery darts of the wicked.

And take the helmet of salvation, and the sword of the Spirit, which is the word of God:

Praying always with all prayer and supplication in the Spirit. . . .[55]

Not only do our children need to understand truth and righteousness, faith and salvation, they need to be familiar with the scriptures, have daily prayer, and understand how God blesses His children when they obey Him. As they get older they need to be taught and reminded often about the darkness and wickedness in the world today. Once they encounter that darkness for themselves, warnings may be too late. Preparing them ahead of time is the key. If they know what to watch for, they will be prepared rather than confused. It takes time to acquire the armor of God. Make sure they are protected and prepared as they go out into the world. Stay close by as they grow to reinforce, remind, and assist, but also to love, encourage, and cheer their good choices.

We need to help our children acquire God's armor as we work on arming ourselves. Our children need to see our testimonies in action in the way we stand up to the evil in the world. It might not always be obvious they are watching us, especially when they make wrong choices, but eventually the results will prove it. Our children cannot fight the power of the adversary alone. Our Heavenly Father gave children something very important He knew could help them withstand the darkness in this world: parents . . . us. It's our responsibility to help prepare them for whatever happens. This is our mandate straight from God. As parents in the gospel, we are to discipline, teach, and prepare them to go into the world and work out their salvation.[56] A strong testimony and a good understanding of the gospel are the best defense our children can have for themselves and for their future children.

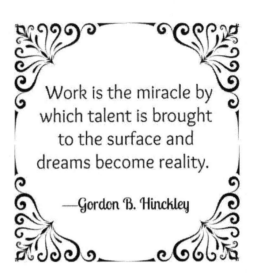

Work is the miracle by
which talent is brought
to the surface and
dreams become reality.

—Gordon B. Hinckley

Work and Its Hidden Blessing: Service

From the very beginning, even while in their garden, Adam and Eve were given a commandment to work, "And the Lord God took the man, and put him into the Garden of Eden to dress it and to keep it."[57]

On leaving the Garden, the commandment to work was ratcheted up a notch:

> In the sweat of thy face shalt thou eat bread, till thou return unto the ground; for out of it wast thou taken: for dust thou art, and unto dust shalt thou return.[58]

Even one of the Ten Commandments is about work. We think of it as only about keeping the Sabbath Day holy and it is. But it also gives guidance for the rest of the week: one day we are to rest but six days we are commanded to work:

> Remember the Sabbath day, to keep it holy.
> Six days shalt thou labour, and do all they work:

But the seventh day is the Sabbath of the Lord thy God: in it thou shalt not do any work. . . .[59]

Scriptures which speak of the Millennium also mention work:

They shall not build, and another inhabit; they shall not plant, and another eat: for as the days of a tree are the days of my people, and mine elect shall long enjoy the work of their hands.[60]

Heavenly Father always intended for work to be a part of our earthly experience. Even He works, "For behold, this is my work and my glory—to bring to pass the immortality and eternal life of man."[61] He told Moses we're His work. If He has emphasized work so much, is it possible to return to Him without learning to work hard?

"Missionary work," "temple work," "family history work," "the work of salvation," "Relief Society's sacred work," and "hasten the work" are just a few areas when church leaders use the term work. Work is beginning to appear inevitable. Why? What is it about hard work that is good for the human soul? What does our Heavenly Father understand about hard work and human nature? Bishop H. David Burton gives us some ideas to consider:

As with any other commandment, there is joy in its keeping. To work—honestly and productively— brings contentment and a sense of self-worth. Having done all we can to be self-reliant, to provide for our own needs and those of our family, we can turn to the Lord in confidence to ask for what we might yet lack.[62]

From God's obvious insistence on the importance of work, perhaps we just need to trust Him and follow His guidance. Yet despite how a good work ethic always has been considered necessary for success, it is quickly becoming a lost art. Parents may think they are doing their kids a favor by not requiring them to work; it's what we all wished for when we were young. It seems much easier and less stressful to just let children play all day, but in reality it is theft. We are stealing from our children the very things that can help them become great, responsible adults: their self-worth and self-reliance.

We cannot take away the concept of work with all its benefits and remain strong individuals, families, or communities. By not passing on a good work ethic to the next generation, society will lose those benefits and pay a hefty price. This is already visible in other countries where hard work is not supported and it's beginning to be seen here as well.

> Genius is 1% talent and 99% percent hard work. . . .
> —Albert Einstein

Part of the work children did in earlier times meant the difference between having a warm or cold house and whether there was enough food to eat. Children were needed for survival in past generations. Now their jobs may seem trivial or unnecessary in comparison, but that can change.

When we first teach small children to do a job, it takes more effort than if we do it ourselves. Whatever the job is, we usually have to do it over anyway. But at a young age, they're very excited to help and that makes a huge difference. As they practice different tasks, their skills improve. They really can do the job better each time until they do it well. That's when a parent's rewards come. Work around the home will be much easier with everyone helping.

81

Work needs to fit the age and abilities of each child. No matter what age, children will need help at first with good directions and oversight. Plan on explaining a few times and then keeping close tabs for a while. Give them specific guidelines and instructions as to what they need to do to accomplish each task, then expect them to follow those guidelines. A schedule and lots of reminders help as well: pick up toys every day before bedtime, vacuum every Saturday, or make breakfast every Thursday morning. This helps kids know what to expect and gives them stability. Their jobs need to increase in breadth and depth as they age and mature. Older siblings can pass their old jobs on to younger ones by teaching them the way mom or dad want it done because, by now, they're pros.

Jobs little children can handle around age three: throw garbage away, bring garbage cans from others rooms to empty, pick up toys, bring something to mom and dad like baby diapers or the phone, keep younger ones occupied, set the table with forks and spoons, match socks in the clean laundry, and make their beds in the morning. Jobs become increasingly harder through the years till as teens they can prepare meals, clean bathrooms, do laundry, mop, dust, vacuum, and pretty much everything else. Dad can teach them car care, yard care, and home repairs along the way. Learning to work will prepare them for a mission, marriage, or moving out on their own.

In our family, we've dedicated one day each week to housework and practical life skills. I've found our weeks go so much more smoothly when our home is in order and my children take pride in knowing THEY helped. Honestly sometimes they complain, but more often than not, they like to help with dusting, scrubbing, making beds, folding, etc.

I feel like we learn sometimes even more on this day than we do other days because we are learning life skills that are becoming habits. These habits will be things they will hopefully carry into adulthood.

To be more specific, my 3- and 5-year-olds do these things: Food prep: scrubbing veggies, chopping, mashing, mixing, scooping, pouring, setting the table, unloading the dishwasher or sorting utensils. Laundry: fold towels, put away clothes, dust, sweep small things with a hand broom, scrub the shower, and make beds. Also, water plants, wipe down chairs, or wipe down base boards.

We don't do all those things every week, but they are capable of doing them when they are asked. The 3-year-old takes a lot longer but I practice my patience in guiding him and not rushing him.

Never discount the importance of these tasks; it helps them feel responsible, successful, and a necessary part of the family. Always thank them after they complete the job properly. Let them know their help contributes to the home running smoothly. Children like to feel needed, and when they are, they will respond. It makes a big difference when kids are seen as an asset and not a liability.

Making jobs into a game can also be helpful. Here are two examples:

Our family assisted some elderly neighbors rake and bag leaves. Rather than just work at it, we decided to see how many bags we could fill in one hour. That made the kids move. We got many more bags filled than if we had just done the work without the game.

When our kids were little, my goal was to have them pick up the toys before dinner and again at bedtime if needed. It was always much easier if I told them I would time them to see if they could do it in less than 5 minutes or if we had a race to see who picked up their part first. That really helped. Making things fun, even in small ways, helps.

Family projects are a great way to teach kids about work. This is when the family all works together doing a bigger job such as weeding the garden, cleaning the garage, or doing projects for neighbors, church, or even a project that brings in some extra money. Everyone helps and the job gets done quickly. These projects can be fun and filled with laughter, stories, jokes, and good conversations. They can become a favorite memory for children. Having treats after a big project is always a child pleaser as well; if someone makes those treats, there is another skill learned.

If children want something and earning the money themselves is not a possibility, give them some jobs they can do to help "pay" for it.

My daughter saw a cute little fur-lined, pink jacket when she was ten or eleven and immediately had to have it. She didn't really need it so I wouldn't buy it for her but I told her she could save up her money and get it herself. She did extra work around the house and saved it all. In a month or so, she had enough. She was very proud as we went to the store where she pulled her own money out of her purse and bought the jacket. A few months later at a practice, she lost it. I have never seen her work so hard to find something. It was obvious that jacket meant something to her because she worked hard to earn it.

Work can bring a great sense of accomplishment. It helps everyone involved be better prepared to handle those unexpected bumps in life which inevitably appear. It gives us the ability to rely on ourselves and our families helping us be more independent. When a trial does arise, we can gather our children around us—those old enough to understand—explain the situation, and ask for their help. Children will rally around, help each other, and work hard to make it through tough times, especially when they know mom and dad are depending on them.

> For even when we were with you, this we commanded you; that if any would not work, neither should he eat.
> — 2 Thess. 3:10

President Dean Jarman, after describing some of his family's work projects in a 1982 conference address, added some principles his sons told him they learned from those experiences:

'They have shaped my character and personality.'

'The harder you work, the better you feel.'

'Family projects taught us the importance of being honest and dependable.'

'When I buy my clothes and other things, I take care of them because I know how much they cost and how much work it takes to buy them. When my parents bought my things, I honestly thought there was an endless supply of money, so I wouldn't take care of them. Also, work gives me a feeling of satisfaction.'[63]

It's hard to teach children to work, but that endeavor on our part as parents will pay off in the long run when our children become good, hard working adults. As kids find their passions, their hard work skills can help change those dreams into reality.

Another benefit of hard work is the way it helps overcome a lack of natural talents, education, or experience. Any boss knows someone who works hard is a better employee than someone who has a lot of talent and no work ethic. Successful people often speak of the long hours and hard work involved in their success, but there are numerous gifted people who never get far because they won't work hard. Coaches quickly figure this out:

My son's basketball coach always has his first tryout scheduled for 5:30 am. He told the boys he didn't want kids on the team who weren't willing to put in the effort. He understands the value of hard work and those who get up early prove they understand it as well.

According to Bishop Burton, teaching our children how to work hard needs to be a specific purpose for Intentional Parents:

One of parents' most important responsibilities is to teach their children to work. Even young children can begin to experience the benefits of working when they are involved in household chores and in service to others. Wise parents will work alongside their children, will provide frequent praise, and will make sure no task is overwhelming.[64]

Bishop Burton mentions the exact reason why I have combined service with work in this chapter. Service gives parents another avenue to teach their children to work and takes away the triviality of other jobs kids might do. Nothing trumps service opportunities for bringing the blessings of work to children and parents alike. And nothing includes the blessings of service like work. Service actually has a role in many household jobs. In a family, work is seldom done just to benefit one person; very often, it benefits every member of the family. Washing dishes, setting the table, cleaning up the toys, or mowing the lawn all benefit the entire family. Jobs like these give our children work but also help them serve their families. It's good to point out this fact when they do these tasks. Often service to others involves work: helping a family move, shoveling sidewalks for an elderly couple, or babysitting the neighbor's kids while their mom runs an errand are some examples. Rather than separating work and service, utilizing their close relationship will ensure a better understanding of both these principles.

Another great way to work and serve is when older children help younger ones with different tasks. They will feel a sense of pride and an increase in love as they help their younger siblings. Having older kids assist their younger siblings with school work such as math or reading will help cement these concepts for the older one as well. Both end up learning while mom and dad get some much needed help. Older siblings can also watch younger ones giving parents time to fix dinner or do other important tasks. These ideas teach service, responsibility, and leadership skills while ensuring an interest in their younger sibling's success.

Serving each other within the family is the first step in learning to truly serve others everywhere, and serving others is the goal we were all given:

And the King shall answer and say unto them, Verily I say unto you, Inasmuch as ye have done it unto one of the least of these my brethren, ye have done it unto me.[65]

It's amazing the options parents can come up with to help their children learn how to work hard *and* serve. Work which helps others has many benefits. Service helps children feel grateful for all they have, it helps them think of other's needs rather than their own, and it helps open their eyes to what's going on around them. Service also teaches compassion, love, and understanding like nothing else can. It can even help a grumpy teen or pre-teen feel happy and cheerful once again. Service projects, big or small, for the entire family to work on together should be a regular part of every home. Encourage children to think of ideas for these family service projects. They love it when it's their idea. It's amazing how serving others brings a family together.

Right before Christmas one year, we heard of a family who lost their home in a fire. Everything was gone. Our children were really sobered to realize this family would have no Christmas, no gifts, no tree, no decorations of any kind, and none of their old things. Their house was a black charred shell. We gathered our children around us, told them our idea to help, and asked if they wanted to join us. We decided on an amount we could afford and our children contributed some of their own money to our stash as well. Then we went to the store and purchased items we knew every family in their situation would need and even a few fun items too. After leaving everything on the doorstep of their newly rented, very empty, apartment, we rang the doorbell and quickly left. Each of our children was thinking how grateful they were for their toys, clothes, belongings and home. They were very grateful that Christmas for all their blessings and also for being able to help a family that really needed it.

Helping others benefits the giver as much as the receiver. It gives us all perspective as well as increased gratitude. I've never seen someone really participate in actual service and not come away changed from the experience. Sometimes teens might act like they don't care since it wouldn't look cool, but they are feeling it too. When they become accustomed to serving others, it transforms a part of them just like other good habits. It is amazing how much of an eye opener it is for kids, who think they have it rough, to see some true poverty. It can really change them; their lives won't be the same again.

Serving others helps us love them. As parents, we love our children because we have served them since they were born. Missionaries learn to love the people in their areas because they serve them. Service—with its associated hard work—opens our hearts to see others as children of God. Families who learn to work and serve each other are closer, happier, and stronger. These are all goals Intentional Parents want for their children. And it all stems from hard work. I think President David O. McKay said it best, "Let us realize that the privilege to work is a gift, that power to work is a blessing, that love of work is success." [66]

Neither age nor size
makes a man.
It is willingness to accept
responsibility.

—Louis L'amour

Tevye's Traditions

Whenever I think of traditions, I am always reminded of the beginning of the musical, *Fiddler on the Roof*. The father, Tevye, explains all about tradition and what it means to him and his family:

A fiddler on the roof. Sounds crazy, no? But in our little village of Anatevka, you might say every one of us is a fiddler on the roof, trying to scratch out a pleasant, simple tune without breaking his neck. It isn't easy. You may ask, why do we stay up there if it's so dangerous? We stay because Anatevka is our home . . . and how do we keep our balance? That I can tell you in one word . . . tradition.

Because of our traditions, we've kept our balance for many, many years. Here in Anatevka we have traditions for everything . . . how to eat, how to sleep, even, how to wear clothes. For instance, we always keep our heads covered and always wear a little prayer shawl. . . . This shows our constant devotion to God. You may ask, how did this tradition start? I'll tell you—I don't know. But it's a tradition. . . . Because of our traditions, everyone knows who he is and what God expects him to do.[67]

That is an amazing thing to say! Can traditions really do all that? Since traditions are about passing experiences, beliefs, and ideas from one generation to the next, it really could be a possibility.

To examine some past traditions and see how they worked, we can look at examples in the scriptures. In the *Book of Mormon,* traditions are spoken of regularly. The influence they exert in these stories is very dramatic—for good and bad. The Nephite traditions included stories about their ancestors, their history, and how they got to the Promised Land. These stories were part of their belief system and reminded them of God and His great blessings. Nephite traditions along with scripture helped convince them to believe in God:

> And thousands were brought to the knowledge of the Lord, yea, thousands were brought to believe in the traditions of the Nephites; and they were taught the records and prophecies which were handed down even to the present time.[68]

This didn't happen just once; the Nephites often used traditions to teach and reinforce gospel principles:

> And it came to pass that whosoever would not believe in the tradition of the Lamanites, but believed those records which were brought out of the land of Jerusalem, and also in the tradition of their fathers, which were correct, who believed in the commandments of God and kept them, were called the Nephites, or the people of Nephi, from that time forth—[69]

Including "would not believe" illustrates it was a choice; they chose which traditions they would believe. We also

92

know it was a choice because they had agency just like we do. We won't ever know the specifics of what was behind their choice to believe or not, but knowing agency exists today, we need to do all we can to help our children make this choice to believe in God and keep His commandments. Can traditions really help with that?

Human beings crave order and hope; they desire purpose and predictability. All these needs can be influenced and nourished by traditions. That's why the Nephites referred to them so frequently. Traditions have a powerful effect; we often see this in our own children. It makes sense to try and harness that power as a way to help their faith and strengthen their budding testimonies.

Unlike the Nephites, the Lamanites used traditions in an entirely opposite way. They taught their children how Nephi stole the government, the Liahona, and the Brass Plates from them. They believed they were rightfully theirs. Through traditions, their descendents learned to hate the Nephites to the degree that it caused fighting and bloodshed between the Lamanites and Nephites for almost a thousand years:

> They were a wild, and ferocious, and a blood-thirsty people, believing in the tradition of their fathers, which is this—Believing that they were driven out of the land of Jerusalem because of the iniquities of their fathers, and that they were wronged in the wilderness by their brethren, and they were also wronged while crossing the sea;
> And again, that they were wronged while in the land of their first inheritance, after they had crossed the sea. . . .
> . . .
> And again, they were wroth with him when they had arrived in the promised land, because they said

that he had taken the ruling of the people out of their hands. . . .

And again, they were wroth with him because he departed into the wilderness as the Lord had commanded him, and took the records which were engraven on the plates of brass, for they said that he robbed them.

And thus they have taught their children that they should hate them, and that they should murder them, and that they should rob and plunder them, and do all they could to destroy them; therefore they have an eternal hatred towards the children of Nephi.[70]

There are destructive family traditions in every age. Shakespeare's *Romeo and Juliet* is very powerful because it speaks to this reality of human nature as well. This type of tradition needs to be replaced with those which promote love, understanding, and forgiveness. The *Book of Mormon* shows the consequences of hate and revenge as clearly as Shakespeare.

The place we can begin to fix this is in our own homes and within our own families. We can learn how tradition can be deep and meaningful or full of lies and wickedness. Understanding these stories of hate and revenge, with all their consequences, brings a newfound respect for the power of traditions. Reading and discussing them should be part of our family teaching moments to help children absorb the lessons of history.

A third example of the way tradition is used in the scriptures takes place in the New Testament. The Jews of Christ's day used many traditions in their families and communities. However, Christ pointed out some problems with their traditions:

[Jesus] answered and said unto them, Well hath Esaias prophesied of you hypocrites, as it is written, This people honoureth me with their lips, but their heart is far from me.

Howbeit in vain do they worship me, teaching for doctrines the commandments of men.

For laying aside the commandment of God, ye hold the tradition of men, as the washing of pots and cups: and many other such like things ye do.

And he said unto them, Full well ye reject the commandment of God, that ye may keep your own tradition.[71]

This is another facet of tradition Intentional Parents need to be aware of. Traditions can be fun and entertaining, but they can also be at odds with commandments and doctrine. Fun, uplifting, *and* faith-promoting traditions are the goal. It may take some creativity, but it is possible to have fun traditions which also stay true to the faith.

We can see from these scriptures just how much power there is in traditions. If they can get one group of people to hate another group for generations, can they also help a generation love God? Can traditions outweigh some of the worldly influences which pull our children away from the gospel? They certainly can't hurt if we use them right. Moses understood this also and tried to set up good traditions for the Children of Israel to follow:

When all Israel is come to appear before the Lord thy God in the place which he shall choose, thou shalt read this law before all Israel in their hearing.

Gather the people together, men, and women, and children, and thy stranger that is within thy gates, that they may hear, and that they may learn, and fear the Lord your God, and observe to do all the words of this law:

And that their children, which have not known anything, may hear, and learn to fear the Lord your God, as long as ye live in the land whither ye go over Jordan to possess it.[72]

Moses knew the outcome he wanted for the people. He realized if they heard the scriptures, their law, read regularly, their testimonies would grow stronger and perhaps they would remain faithful. It's the same reason why our church leaders want us to read and study the scriptures daily. If this idea had become the tradition Moses meant it to be, the history of the Children of Israel may have turned out very differently. Moses had goals he wanted for the people and he very intentionally taught them traditions which had the potential to help them reach those goals. But their children and especially their children's children didn't keep the traditions going; those future generations did not become Intentional Parents for their children and consequently those generations slowly fell into apostasy.

> If you want your children to turn out well, spend twice as much time with them and half as much money.
> — Abigail Van Buren

When I think of today's traditions, I can see three different levels of depth. The first is a level where traditions are all about fun: a Thanksgiving turkey, Christmas trees covered in decorations, and Easter egg hunts, just to name a few. Along with these fun ones are those which fill a deeper level of tradition. They help us with our responsibilities as we work on raising our children. Many families have a bedtime ritual to help get children in bed. Doing the same routine every night calms them and helps them prepare for sleeping. Our bedtime ritual is simple: clean up the toys, get ready for bed, mom reads stories, and then dad helps them say prayers and tucks them in. It really has helped wind down the evening peacefully in our home.

The third and deepest level would be Tevye's type. These traditions might include special family night lessons for Christmas, Thanksgiving, and Easter every year. Rather than getting tired of them, children are excited to hear these familiar stories each year. Sometimes old family recipes handed down from grandparents and great-grandparents are part of this level. Another example might be the way a family does their family nights or their family service projects.

> *One tradition we have in our family is our Thanksgiving Jar. A few times during the year as part of family night, we each write things we are grateful for on slips of paper and place them in the jar. On the family night before Thanksgiving we open it and take turns reading the notes. Some are funny and some are serious but all of them remind us of the wonderful things which happened throughout the year. A few of the notes remind us of things we have totally forgotten; we would never remember all those blessings without our Thanksgiving Jar. It really helps our family recall all the reasons we have to be grateful on Thanksgiving and throughout the year.*

This family tradition is fun and easy while at the same time it helps children learn gratitude by seeing just how blessed they are. Imagine kids thinking of all the things they are grateful for. What a great spirit this will bring into our homes.

Traditions can be about a lot more than simply making fun memories; they can also teach children about their place within their families and in the world, help give kids stability as well as a strong foundation, and help define their relationship with God. Traditions in this deepest level can help us raise our children in the gospel and strengthen their faith. Through them, our children discover why we believe what we do and how it affects us individually.

Learning stories of ancestors is a great way to give children perspective for their own life. Stories of their challenges and the hard work it took to overcome those can be very powerful. But it all has to start with getting to know those ancestors:

My mother's family is from Italy and her parents brought an Italian tradition with them when they immigrated to the United States. A few weeks before Christmas, our family gathers around the kitchen table and we all make special stuffed pasta, called Cappelletti, for our Christmas dinner. We make the pasta in advance and freeze it until Christmas Day. The process of making the dough, rolling it out really thin, cutting it, filling it, and sealing it takes about 3-4 hours to make enough to feed our family. Everyone knows we all participate and as kids we didn't mind at all! We only had this dish once a year and it was our favorite!

While our family sits around the table for several hours making pasta, we tell jokes, listen to family stories and really have wonderful opportunities to re-connect with each other. I will always remember the times when my grandmother was around to help us make Cappelletti. She was only 4' 10". She had a rolling pin that my grandfather made for her and it was almost as long as she was tall. Grandma could roll that dough out very thin without tearing the pasta, which isn't an easy thing to do. There was a certain "slapping" sound that the dough would make as she turned it over on the table. That sound is how you knew the dough was just the right texture: not too wet and not too dry.

While we were stuffing and sealing pasta, Grandma would tell us stories of when she was a young girl. Her family ran a boarding house and it was her job every Tuesday to make all the pasta her family and the boarders would eat for the week. Grandma told us she was so short she had to stand on a wooden crate to reach the counter. She made a lot of pasta in her 94 years of life.

My grandmother has been gone now for many years. My own mother is gone as well, and I still gather my children around my kitchen table each December and we make Cappelletti. I talk to my children about current events, and we tell jokes. We talk about our memories of my mother and grandmother as we make this dish that has been handed down from generation to generation, from mother to daughter for at least 150 years. We love the memories we have made over the years and the links to previous generations this has created as we carry on this tradition.

What an amazing tradition which helps this family cement their relationships and teaches their children the wonderful heritage with which our Heavenly Father has blessed them. It's surprising how fun traditions can be while still accomplishing the goals we have as Intentional Parents. We may not have great Italian pasta in our heritage but that doesn't mean we can't start our own fun, new tradition which can accomplish great things too.

As we pick rituals and traditions for our families, we can intentionally plan ahead for what we want those traditions to teach our children: traditions which will create a happier home, teach them good principles, and, most importantly, increase their faith and understanding of our Heavenly Father and Jesus Christ.

As we intentionally choose our family traditions to include those that will also strengthen our children in the gospel, we can then say along with Tevye, "Because of our traditions, everyone knows who he is and what God expects him to do."[73]

Here are a few more family traditions. Hopefully they can spark some imagination for you:

We have a Family History Minute every Family Home Evening night as part of the rotating assignments. It can be something a child remembers doing with the family, memories from recent or long ago, or a short story from anyone in our family history: parents, grandparents, great-grand parents, etc.

Every year at our annual family reunion my husband's grandmother tells a couple stories about ancestors. This year for each of the kid's birthdays she wrote those stories down and made a notebook for each of the kids with the stories inside so they can learn them. They are written as bedtime stories and are pretty short.

We visit cemeteries. The children joke about it and say that their parents vacation with dead people, but it gives us time to talk about and remember our ancestors. We tour the towns they lived in and, when we meet people, we wonder if they are distant cousins.

We emphasize the importance of taking the sacrament at church each week. Even when they were little, no books or crayons were allowed until after the sacrament. Freely talking about our love for the Savior has become a pattern of speech in our home.

We have a book of artwork with the words to "The Living Christ" (phrase by phrase), and especially during the summer we add that to our devotional time, reading/ memorizing it all together—actually, this summer we interspersed with "The Family A Proclamation to the World" from day to day.

We do things through the season, but here's our Christmas day tradition: Christmas morning kids can get up any time after 6 a.m., BUT they can only get into their Christmas stockings. The rest of us are usually up by 7, and we start with a Christmas hymn and family prayer, then read Luke chapter 2, using lots of pictures and a couple hymns that fit as we go. Afterwards we take turns each opening one present, and go enjoy it and breakfast. We open one present each per hour plus one family gift on the hour; this helps everyone be more reflective and grateful AND have a chance to spend time with each gift instead of throwing it to the side in pursuit of the next. (If we're not done by 1:00, we usually open the rest then.) And then we call parents, grandparents, and whoever sent gifts and talk with them.

We do our Christmas morning almost the same way [as the one above]. The one thing we do additionally is before anyone can open another gift they have to say something they are grateful for and why.

What will your family's new faith promoting tradition be?

Just Begin
Where You Are

If we work upon marble, it will perish; if we work
upon brass, time will efface it; if we rear temples,
they will crumble to dust; but if we work on men's
immortal minds, if we impress on them with high
principles, the just fear of God and love for their
fellow-men, we engrave on those tablets something
which no time can efface, and which will brighten
and brighten to all eternity.[74]

— Daniel Webster

I'm guessing some chapters or topics have felt
overwhelming or, at least, not specific enough. It's entirely
possible that many of these chapters have been annoyingly
vague. If so, I understand the frustration; but that was my
intention. By no means is this meant to replace the
inspiration every parent can receive straight from God;
which is much better than some old book giving step-by-
step instructions. Not only is each child very unique,
making a one-size-fits-all plan impossible, there really is no
such thing as an easy answer when it comes to raising
children. However, we can rely on our Father in Heaven for
help. We are promised His help and guidance as long as we

remain faithful. He can and will inspire us with what is best in each situation if we do our part. We are not embracing Intentional Parenting because it's fun or easy. We believe in Intentional Parenting because our children are worth it and because God has given us that responsibility:

> The home is the first and most effective place for children to learn the lessons of life: truth, honor, virtue, self-control; the value of education, honest work, and the purpose and privilege of life. Nothing can take the place of home in rearing and teaching children, and no other success can compensate for failure in the home.[75]

Most everyone will recognize this last line as President David O. McKay's famous quote, but few have heard the entire paragraph teaching the principles necessary for Intentional Parenting. Families and parenting have been a part of the Father's plan from the beginning:

> God, our Heavenly Father, is a family man, and he believes in families. If you don't think so, just look around you. We all belong to him. We are his family, and all of the great blessings that he has in store for his children will come through families. They don't come any other way. Of course, all of his children who are worthy will have the opportunity to have this blessing. Exaltation is a family affair, and so we build temples . . . but temples are *family* houses. They are set apart to create families for all eternity. . . . That is the great purpose, the work and the glory of our Father in heaven. He believes in families.[76]

Intentional Parenting can sometimes feel overwhelming. It's easy to look back at these chapters with all the information presented and give up before we even begin. Or maybe we may think, "If I were a new parent I could do it, but it's just too late now." This doesn't sound like inspiration from the Lord to me.

We can't let discouragement stop us from trying. Rather than giving up, remember it's all about starting small. Prayerfully pick one thing to work on first; maybe a new tradition for a holiday coming up or maybe just being better about having family night regularly or following

> Love is unselfishly choosing for another's highest good.
> — C. S. Lewis

through with rules. It's amazing what even a small change can accomplish. Once that's going well, try adding something else. As we tackle a big project one bite at a time, it's incredible how blessings start to flow. Heavenly Father doesn't expect us to run faster than we are able,[77] but I do think He expects us to try our hardest. When we do, He blesses us with more stamina, patience, or whatever we need. He won't make it easy but He does help us get through it. We will reach the other side better, stronger, and more faithful for having tried. Don't let it seem overwhelming by picturing it all at once. Just take that first tiny step.

Fathers and mothers, it is not too late to change. There is still hope. You can begin today to apply these suggestions and others you may add. We can help our children and grandchildren to survive spiritually and morally in a world where the pollution index continues to spiral upward.[78]

Elder Joe J. Christensen said this in 1993. Today's moral pollution index is much worse. Since it will only continue to increase, it's important to do whatever we can to help our children get all the extra oil their lamps will need.[79] They will have to be strong on their own and for their children. I don't want to look back as a grandparent and wish I had done more. My precious, future grandchildren are too important. I need my children to be Intentional Parents for their sakes and it's my job to raise them to be those future Intentional Parents.

> *Perhaps God was talking to my family when He said, "The weak things of the world shall come forth and break down the mighty and strong ones, that man should not counsel his fellow man, neither trust in the arm of flesh."[80] We definitely fit the description of "the weak things of the world," but as we develop faith to inquire of the Lord and trust in His directions, we are led to not only know what is right, but we are also strengthened to do what may seem against the wisdom of the world. Being intentional in our parenting and trusting in God gives us power that the arm of flesh could never deliver.*

The goal of this book is to pass on the vision and principles of Intentional Parenting and then leave the rest to Intentional Parents and God. Parents, doing their best to help their children as they live the gospel, have been promised God's help if they ask, listen, and keep moving forward while doing the best they can. We are given no guarantees our children won't choose another path as adults, but Intentional Parenting keeps us focused on the long term rather than getting easily distracted by less important things.

106

Elder Bradley D. Foster told a story of a father who was an Intentional Parent:

"When I was nine, my dad took me aside and said, 'Pablo, I was nine once too. Here are some things you may come across. You'll see people cheating in school. You might be around people who swear. You'll probably have days when you don't want to go to church. Now, when these things happen—or anything else that troubles you—I want you to come and talk to me, and I'll help you get through them. And then I'll tell you what comes next.'"

"So, Pablo, what did he tell you when you were 10?"

"Well, he warned me about pornography and dirty jokes."

"What about when you were 11?" I asked.

"He cautioned me about things that could be addictive and reminded me about using my agency."

Here was a father, year after year . . . who helped his son not only hear but also understand. Pablo's father knew our children learn when they are ready to learn, not just when we are ready to teach them.[81]

Pablo's story is a great example of Intentional Parenting. Was Pablo's father perfect? No. Did he always remember to do everything on his "father" list? Most likely, no. But he never stopped trying his best, and that's the key! As Intentional Parents, we pick ourselves up after each mistake, dust ourselves off, and keep going. Perfection is not required; we just need to keep working at it. God's grace is there for parents too.

As the world careens further and further away from the family and its God-given mandate to raise His children in faith, we must gather together and form a united front to protect our families. It might feel like we're on our own, but we're not. We may falter or feel as though we are losing our footing; but with God on our side, He will make up any part we may lack. If we stand with Him for our families and for truth, we have been promised His blessings and help. Families have been central to God's plan from the beginning. Everything in the gospel is built around the family and how to strengthen it.

> Children are not a distraction from more important work. They are the most important work.
> — C. S. Lewis

It's common to feel something like, "It was easy for Nephi, he was a prophet" when we read about these people who gave their all. However, I think that might be looking at it backwards. Nephi became a prophet because of his faith and willingness to do hard things. He didn't become a prophet and then the hard things became easy. As I read Nephi's story, I never get the feeling the ship was easy to build, it was a simple thing to get the plates from Laban, or even that it was almost a vacation traveling in the wilderness for so many years.

Just like Nephi's work, Intentional Parenting is a challenge; but then so is everything worth doing. If Nephi could build a ship, if Joseph Smith could translate the plates and found the church, if Esther could save her people from eminent destruction, and if Hannah could give her only son to the Lord, then we can all become Intentional Parents and work to raise future Intentional Parents. We have the same spiritual channels and the same potential blessings as they did. What we need is the faith to take that first step. We might find other parents want to gather with us and to help each other in our challenges. It takes just one person or family willing to begin and then others will join. We can be the beginning of a movement returning families to their original purpose.

Intentional Parents are trying to accomplish the Lord's work and are therefore promised help and direction. If we do our part, these promises are truly miraculous. Here is one example from a talk by Elder Russell M. Nelson:

> Today, let me add that we need women who know how to make important things happen by their faith and who are courageous defenders of morality and families in a sin-sick world. We need women who are devoted to shepherding God's children along the covenant path toward exaltation; women who know how to receive personal revelation; who understand the power and peace of the temple endowment, women who know how to call upon the powers of heaven to protect and strengthen children and families.
>
> . . . And I promise you in the name of Jesus Christ that as you do so, the Holy Ghost will magnify your influence in an unprecedented way![82]

This is what we are all striving for. In a world that scoffs at faith and rejects heaven altogether, it's easy to mistrust our own beliefs about personal revelation. As we raise future Intentional Parents, we need to trust in the words of our leaders and start to exhibit more faith in a Father in Heaven who has shown us how much He cares and how much He wants to help. Let's accept His help! Through the guidance of His Spirit, we can help transform this earth one child and one family at a time.

Let us continue,
brethren and sisters,
to work in the name of
the Lord our God;
gathering wisdom and
intelligence day by day,
that every circumstance which
transpires may
minister to our good.
—Lorenzo Snow

Resources

GatheringFamilies.com – a gathering place for Intentional Parents
Church – This is a great place to find parents to talk with, an older successful parent for a mentor, or most importantly, help from God.
Mentors – Find someone who is an experienced, successful parent.
Watch and learn from them. Don't be afraid to ask questions; most people usually like to share stories of their successes.

Conference and BYU talks:
(This list is only a partial list of many great talks given on parenting and families.)

- "Like a Flame Unquenchable" by M. Russell Ballard
- "The Sacred Responsibilities of Parenthood" by M. Russell Ballard
- "Learning to Love Learning" by David A. Bednar
- "To the Mothers in Zion" by Ezra Taft Benson
- "To the Fathers in Israel" by Ezra Taft Benson
- "The Blessing of Work" by H. David Burton

- "Marriage and the Great Plan of Happiness" by Joe J. Christensen
- "Rearing Children in a Polluted Environment" by Joe J. Christensen
- "A Table Encircled with Love" by LeGrand R. Curtis
- "That We May Be One" by Henry B. Eyring
- "The Greatest Challenge in the World—Good Parenting" by James E. Faust
- "Strengthening Families: Our Sacred Duty" by Robert D. Hales
- "With All the Feeling of a Tender Parent: A Message of Hope to Families" by Robert D. Hales
- "Of You It Is Required to Forgive" by Gordon B. Hinckley
- "The Blessings of Family Prayer" by Gordon B. Hinckley
- "Because She Is a Mother" by Jeffrey R. Holland
- "Oneness in Marriage" by Spencer W. Kimball
- "Set Some Personal Goals," by Spencer W. Kimball
- "The Role of Righteous Women." By Spencer W. Kimball
- "Train Up a Child" by Spencer W. Kimball
- "Precious Children, A Gift from God" by Thomas S. Monson
- "A Plea to My Sisters" by Russell M. Nelson
- "For Time and All Eternity" by Boyd K. Packer
- "Teach the Children" by Boyd K. Packer
- "Prepare Yourself to Raise a Family in the Lord" by Hartman Rector Jr.
- "Agency and Anger" by Lynn G. Robbins
- "Finding Joy in Life" by Richard G. Scott
- "Marriage and Family: Our Sacred Responsibility" by W. Douglas Shumway

- "Constancy and Change" by N. Eldon Tanner
- "Patience, a Key to Happiness" by Joseph B. Wirthlin

Classics Books:

Laddie by Gene Stratton Porter
Little Britches by Ralph Moody
Little Women, Little Men, Jo's Boys, by Louisa May Alcott
Little House on the Prairie series by Laura Ingalls Wilder
Little Bear books by Else Holmelund Minarik

Notes

All italicized stories are anonymous contributions by parents of GatheringFamilies.com

Chapter 1: The Idea of Intentional Parenting

[1] Alma 53:21, 56:47-48, *Book of Mormon,* https://www.lds.org/scriptures/bofm?lang=eng. Accessed 11 Nov. 2016.

[2] Mosiah 26:1-4, *Book of Mormon.*

[3] Telushkin, Joseph. "What Did Your Parents Most Want You to Be?" *YouTube,* uploaded by PragerU, Mar 17, 2014, www.youtube.com/watch?v=5adJxEWLFKU. Accessed 11 Nov. 2016.

[4] Kimball, Spencer W. "The Role of Righteous Women." Oct, 1979, www.lds.org/general-conference/1979/10/the-role-of-righteous-women?lang=eng. Accessed 11 Nov. 2016.

[5] Mckay, Hollie. "Critics Slam MSNBC Host's Claim That Kids Belong to Community, Not Parents," *Fox News Entertainment*, April 9, 2013, www.foxnews.com/entertainment/2013/04/09/critics-slam-msnbc-hosts-claim-that-kids-belong-to-community-not-parents.html. Accessed 11 Nov. 2016.

[6] Clinton, Hillary R. *It Takes A Village*, Simon and Schuster, Jan 1, 1996.

[7] *The Family: A Proclamation to the World,* Sept. 23, 1995, www.lds.org/topics/family-proclamation?lang=eng&_r=1. Accessed 11 Nov. 2016.

[8] Ibid.

[9] Kimball, Spencer W. "The Role of Righteous Women."

[10] Reagan, Ronald. Address to the annual meeting of the Phoenix Chamber of Commerce, 30 March 1961, https://en.wikiquote.org/wiki/Ronald_Reagan. Accessed 11 Nov. 2016.

[11] Jacob 1:19, *Book of Mormon.*

Chapter 2: Preparation for the Unknown

[12] 1 Nephi 3:7, *Book of Mormon.*

[13] 1 Nephi 4:6-7, *Book of Mormon.*

[14] 1 Nephi 17:7-10, *Book of Mormon.*

[15] Doctrine and Covenants 88:118-119, *Doctrine and Covenants,* https://www.lds.org/scriptures/dc-testament?lang=eng. Accessed 11 Nov. 2016.

[16] Genesis 2:24, *The Holy Bible,* Authorized King James Version, https://www.lds.org/scriptures/bible?lang=eng. Accessed 11 Nov. 2016.

[17] Enos 1:1-4, *Book of Mormon.*

[18] Alma 56:47-48, 27, *Book of Mormon.*

[19] *The Family: A Proclamation to the World.*

Chapter 3: Goals: All Shapes and Sizes

[20] Carroll, Lewis, *Alice's Adventures in Wonderland,* 1865, http://www.cat-lovers-gifts-guide.com/cheshire-cat-quotes.html. Accessed 11 Nov. 2016.

[21] 1 Nephi 9:3-6, *Book of Mormon.*

[22] Mosiah 1:4, *Book of Mormon.*

[23] Monson, Thomas S. "To the Rescue," *Ensign,* April 2001, 49, www.lds.org/general-conference/2001/04/to-the-rescue?lang=eng. Accessed 11 Nov. 2016.

[24] Kimball, Spencer W. "Set Some Personal Goals," *Ensign*, April, 1985, www.lds.org/general-conference/1985/04/set-some-personal-goals?lang=eng. Accessed 11 Nov. 2016.

Chapter 4: Raise a Family in the Lord

[25] Rector, Hartman, Jr., "Prepare Yourself to Raise a Family in the Lord," BYU Speeches, Jan 7, 1973, https://speeches.byu.edu/talks/hartman-jr-rector_prepare-raise-family-lord/. Accessed 11 Nov. 2016.

[26] Ibid.

[27] Shumway, W. Douglas. "Marriage and Family: Our Sacred Responsibility," *Ensign*, April, 2004, www.lds.org/general-

conference/2004/04/marriage-and-family-our-sacred-responsibility?lang=eng. Accessed 11 Nov. 2016.

[28] Enos 1:1, *Book of Mormon.*

[29] Kimball, Spencer W. "The Role of Righteous Women."

[30] Lewis, C. S. "Collected Letters of C. S. Lewis," 2006, http://frjohnpeck.com/the-ultimate-career/. Accessed 11 Nov. 2016.

[31] Ballard, M. Russell. "The Sacred Responsibilities of Parenthood," BYU Speeches, August 19, 2003, https://speeches.byu.edu/talks/m-russell-ballard_sacred-responsibilities-parenthood/. Accessed 11 Nov. 2016.

[32] Wirthlin, Joseph B. "Patience, a Key to Happiness," *Ensign*, May 1987, www.lds.org/ensign/1987/05/patience-a-key-to-happiness?lang=eng. Accessed 11 Nov. 2016.

Chapter 5: The Intricacies of Agency

[33] Matthew 15:11, *The Holy Bible.*

[34] 2 Nephi 2:27, *Book of Mormon.*

[35] Alma 42:17-20, *Book of Mormon.*

[36] Proverbs 22:6, *The Holy Bible.*

[37] *Webster's Dictionary 1828 - Online Edition,* http://webstersdictionary1828.com/Dictionary/train. Accessed 11 Nov. 2016.

[38] Kimball, Spencer W. "Train Up a Child." *Ensign*, April, 1978, www.lds.org/ensign/1978/04/train-up-a-child?lang=eng. Accessed 11 Nov. 2016.

[39] Ibid.

[40] Ibid.

Chapter 6: Teaching Moments, Temporal and Eternal

[41] Doctrine and Covenants 97:1.

[42] Bednar, David A. "Learning to Love Learning," BYU Speeches, April 24, 2008, https://speeches.byu.edu/talks/david-a-bednar_learning-love-learning/. Accessed 11 Nov. 2016.

[43] Hales, Robert D. "With All the Feelings of a Tender Parent: A Message of Hope to Families," *Ensign*, April, 2004, www.lds.org/general-conference/2004/04/with-all-the-feeling-of-a-

tender-parent-a-message-of-hope-to-families?lang=eng&_r=1. Accessed 11 Nov. 2016.

[44] Mosiah 1:4, *Book of Mormon.*

[45] Deuteronomy 6:7, *The Holy Bible.*

[46] Doctrine and Covenants 93:36, 40-43.

Chapter 7: Discipline for Future Disciples

[47] Koh, Michael. "30 People Share The Most Creative Punishment They Have Ever Received," *Thought Catalog*, March 7, 2014, https://thoughtcatalog.com/hok-leahcim/2014/03/30-people-share-the-most-creative-punishment-they-have-ever-received/. Accessed 11 Nov. 2016.

[48] Ibid.

[49] *Webster's Dictionary 1828 - Online Edition.*

[50] *Webster's Dictionary 1828 - Online Edition.*

[51] Alma 42:17-18, *Book of Mormon.*

[52] Koh, Michael. "30 People Share The Most Creative Punishment They Have Ever Received."

[53] Ibid.

[54] Ibid.

[55] Ephesians 6:11-18, *The Holy Bible.*

[56] Alma 34:37, *Book of Mormon.*

Chapter 8: Work and Its Hidden Blessing: Service

[57] Genesis 2:15, *The Holy Bible.*

[58] Genesis 3:19, *The Holy Bible.*

[59] Exodus 20:8-10, *The Holy Bible.*

[60] Isaiah 65:22, *The Holy Bible.*

[61] Moses 1:39, *Pearl of Great Price,* https://www.lds.org/scriptures/pgp?lang=eng. Accessed 11 Nov. 2016.

[62] Burton, H. David. "The Blessing of Work," *Ensign*, Dec. 2009, www.lds.org/ensign/2009/12/the-blessing-of-work?lang=eng. Accessed 11 Nov. 2016. Accessed 11 Nov. 2016.

[63] Jarmen, Dean. "The Blessing of Family Work Projects," Ensign, Oct. 1982, https://www.lds.org/general-conference/1982/10/the-blessings-of-family-work-projects?lang=eng. Accessed 11 Nov. 2016.

[64] Burton, H. David. "The Blessing of Work."

[65] Matthew 25:40, *The Holy Bible.*

[66] Burton, H. David. "The Blessing of Work."

Chapter 9: Tevye's Traditions

[67] Stein, Joseph. *Fiddler on the Roof,* 1964, Prologue lyrics. http://www.metrolyrics.com/prologue-lyrics-john-williams.html. Accessed 11 Nov. 2016.

[68] Alma 23:5, *Book of Mormon.*

[69] Alma 3:11, *Book of Mormon.*

[70] Mosiah 10:12-17, *Book of Mormon.*

[71] Mark 7:6-9, *The Holy Bible.*

[72] Deuteronomy 31:11-13, *The Holy Bible.*

[73] Stein, Joseph. *Fiddler on the Roof.*

Chapter 10: Just Begin Where You Are

[74] Address Delivered by the Hon. Daniel Webster in Faneuil Hall, May 22, 1852, at the Request of the City Council of Boston. City Document No. 31. Boston: J.H. Eastburn, 1852. Accessed 11 Nov. 2016.

[75] "Learning Our Duties as Leaders," *Principles of Leadership Teachers Manual Religion 180R*, 2001, 28–32, https://www.lds.org/manual/principles-of-leadership-teachers-manual-religion-180r/learning-our-duties-as-leaders?lang=eng. Accessed 11 Nov. 2016.

[76] Rector, Hartman, Jr., "Prepare Yourself to Raise a Family in the Lord."

[77] Doctrine and Covenants 10:4; Mosiah 4:27, *Book of Mormon.*

[78] Christensen, Joe J. "Rearing Children in a Polluted Environment." *Ensign*, Oct, 1993, www.lds.org/general-conference/1993/10/rearing-children-in-a-polluted-environment?lang=eng. Accessed 11 Nov. 2016.

[79] Matthew 25:1-13, *The Holy Bible.*

[80] Doctrine and Covenants 1:19.

[81] Foster, Bradley D. "It's Never Too Late and It's Never Too Early," *Ensign*, Oct., 2015, www.lds.org/general-conference/2015/10/its-never-too-early-and-its-never-too-late?lang=eng. Accessed 11 Nov. 2016.

[82] Nelson, Russell M. "A Plea to My Sisters," *Ensign*, Oct 2015, www.lds.org/general-conference/2015/10/a-plea-to-my-sisters?lang=eng. Accessed 11 Nov. 2016.

Made in the USA
Columbia, SC
07 August 2019